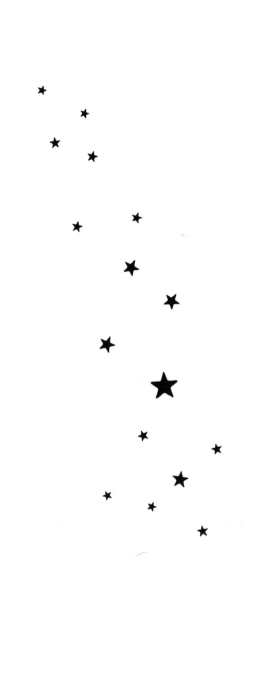

EVOLUTION
OF A
PSYCHIC
By Shirlee Teabo

Single copies available from:

The Sixth Sense
226 South 312th Street
Federal Way, Washington 98003
(206) 839-6281

Discounts available for quantity orders.

FIRST EDITION
March 1984

Library of Congress Catalog Card Number: 83-27398
ISBN: 0-916682-39-0
Library of Congress Cataloging in Publication Data

Teabo, Shirlee, 1933-
Evolution of a psychic.

1. Teabo, Shirlee, 1933-   . 2. Psychical research
—Biography.   I. Title
BF1027.T43A33   1984 133.8[B]   83-27398
ISBN 0-916682-39-0

Published by Outdoor Empire Publishing, Inc.
511 Eastlake Avenue E., P.O. Box C-19000
Seattle, Washington 98109
(206) 624-3845
Printed in the United States of America

This book is lovingly dedicated to.......

Brad and Francie Steiger, who have led the path of Love and Light for others to follow.

Larry Dieffenbach—There are guardian angels that walk this earth, some are highly visible, others like Larry stay in the quiet shadows but are always there with love, support, understanding and help. He is a haven of refuge for so many of us—Thank God for this quiet soul, my friend.

FOREWORD

Evolution of a Psychic is a straightforward, unpretentious—and sometimes wildly humorous—account of
one woman's development into one of this nation's
most accurate and astonishing psychics. It would be by
no small coincidence that its author, Shirlee Teabo, is
herself straightforward, unpretentious—and sometimes
wildly humorous.

Although I have not known Shirlee for a terribly long
period of time, the experiences that we have shared
have definitely been quality happenings. My wife
Frances and I have come to count Shirlee, Bob, Jacquie,
and the Seattle Sixth Sense All-Stars among our dearest friends in the metaphysical community. Although
we all take very seriously our commitment to spread
Light and awareness to all sincere seekers, we have
learned not to take ourselves very seriously; and it has
always been good to unwind with fellow workers in the
Cosmic Gardens who have achieved the balance between spirituality and materiality—and who have
maintained a sense of humor in the process.

Shirlee has consistently kept her sense of humor, as
well as her wits, as she has encountered spirits, spirit
guides, and the intense responsibility of spiritual gifts.
Her devotion to her guide, Xan, becomes a marvelous
model of conduct for all those who desire a serious
partnership with the World Beyond the Physical. Her
acceptance of what others might term misfortunes and
calamities as growth and learning experiences pay

tribute to her absorption of the Higher Plane teachings which Xan has shared with her. And fortunately, Shirlee has chosen to share these same teachings with us.

"You either believe or you disbelieve," Shirlee tells her reader in the opening line of the book. She does not proselytize, but she does, systematically, in a very matter-of-fact way, tend to make belivers out of everyone who has a mind open enough to listen to her reasoned accounts. It must be understood that Shirlee has not been a "believer" all of her life, and she permits the reader to grow into awareness along with her.

Evolution of a Psychic is written in an easy-to-experience, conversational style. I felt very much as if I were sitting with Shirlee, Bob, and the "gang" in their attractive home, listening to this very gifted storyteller speaking in a relaxed manner about revelations, higher awareness, and bizarre things that go bump in the night . . . or in nightclubs . . . or in automobiles . . . or in kitchens.

Shirlee Teabo, I am delighted that you are so happy on your Quest. Thanks for asking us to come along!

Brad Steiger
Scottsdale, Arizona

INTRODUCTION

You either believe or you disbelieve.

We spend our lives sifting sand and searching the furthest limits of the universe for simple truths. Yet none of us are quite sure where to place our faith.

Were the heavens and the earth and all things that inhabit therein created in seven days or did it take billions of years? And is man God's greatest creation or His greatest indiscretion?

Even among saints there are moments of uncertainty and doubt.

And so, when I proclaim myself a psychic, which is a far cry from claiming to receive messages from the Almighty, I expect to be met with doubt and even charges of heresy.

But I wonder, is it heresy to believe in God and at the same time to believe in Man?

In the beginning, I was not a psychic. Or, if I was, I didn't recognize it.

When my best laid plans went somehow awry, I was prone to announce emphatically that I knew this was going to happen. But I doubt that I ever did.

There was nothing exceptional about my childhood, other than that fact that on my 11th birthday, I didn't get a cake because my mother came home from the hospital that day with my newborn sister. I certainly didn't know that was going to happen.

I was the eldest of four children. My sister is the baby

of the family. Between us are two brothers. We got along like most brothers and sisters, which meant it would take years of separation to draw us together.

My father was foreman at a machine shop in Tacoma, Washington. My mother was the quintessential housewife, baking cookies, dabbing at runny noses and generally keeping the home fires burning while my father plied his trade. Only once did Mother escape the rigors of domesticity. I could never decide whether financial exigencies demanded her excursion into the work force or if she was merely running away from home. Perhaps her faith in her children's ability to fend for themselves overcame common sense. If so, reality quickly brought that flight of fancy back to earth.

We accidentally cut off a neighbor girl's toe with a spade. Then we trashed the house in a monumental fight over who was going to clean the kitchen. It culminated in an idle threat I leveled at my sister involving the separation of her head from her shoulder some night when she was deep in sleep.

It all sounded much worse than it really was, but Mother has never been one to take chances. Her apron strings were once more within easy reach.

As a consequence, we were never rich. But then again, we were never poor either. We were what is quaintly referred to as comfortable. And part of that comfort was an endless army of friends of all ages, shapes and sizes who came to dig with us for clams in the soft murk at the base of the cliff on which our house stood at the edge of Puget Sound.

I whiled away my youth perched atop that cliff watching the waves tumble endlessly to shore, wondering where they came from, what strange, exotic places they had seen.

I was waiting for something, but what it was I don't think I ever knew. It had no name, or even a voice. Yet it beckoned.

I have spent my life listening for the siren's call, craning my neck to watch the voices I believe are there.

Maybe it is nothing more than what others have called communion with nature, but if it is, it is a communion Mother has sometimes found disconcerting.

Like Dr. Doolittle, I talk to the animals. And sometimes, they talk back.

My mother now delights in telling complete strangers about the day I danced with the mastiff. Apparently, though she found it less ammusing at the time.

"She was only four," my mother marvels, "just a little bit of a thing. We were living in the country and I took her to town with me to do some shopping."

She grins as she warms to her subject. "We were walking along the sidewalk when this huge dog loomed up in front of us. His head must have been this big," she says, stretching her hands like an aged angler lamenting that one that got away. "I started to pull little Shirlee to me but she gave a shriek and tore away and went running to that giant dog."

"I held my breath. I thought he was going to eat her alive. Instead, he reared up on his hind legs and threw his paws around her neck. They hugged like lost friends while I stood trembling, afraid to say anything. Slowly, I pulled her away and hurried down the street as quickly as my legs would carry us."

I don't recall the incident. And I might even be tempted to chalk it up to an overzealous mother's imagination. But there were other incidents. And these I remember.

I was perhaps eight years old when I started going to day camp at a park in Tacoma. There, several wild animals were kept in cages that lined one of the park's many paths. I would stop each day to talk to the animals, especially my favorites, a lion who had no name and a bear I had christened Ramona.

As I talked aloud, the lion would stare intently into my eyes. She would answer questions with an emotional growl as she kept pace with me walking back and forth in front of her cage.

Ramona was even more demonstrative. "Roll over," I

would plead, and she would clumsily topple onto her side, roll, then scramble back to her feet, rising to her full height to clasp the bars as she watched me giggle affectionately. There was nothing remarkable about talking to the animals. All the kids did it. But only Lion and Ramona responded. And only to me. They ignored the others, who were soon coming to me with tricks they'd like to see.

Then one day, the park officials complained that I was disturbing the animals. Lion had become so tame that they couldn't keep her with the other cats. The sound of our bus arriving each morning was enough to set her off. Lion would roar expectantly and Ramona would stand in the corner of her cage, gazing along the path on which I invariably arrived. On days I didn't show up at all, the animals laid around listlessly, the park officials said, asking that my parents please make sure I didn't talk to the animals anymore.

At first, I was inwardly proud, then embarrassed, then sad. I never went to see Lion or Ramona again.

But the longer I thought of them, the sadder I grew. I had cared for them but had cared in a childish way. They deserved better than the friendship I had been able to offer. They had pleaded with me but I had been unable to hear.

It would be a long time before I would again admit to talking to the animals. Longer still before I would learn to listen.

There is a Bengal tiger in Point Defiance Park in Tacoma who longs for freedom. I know because I have heard him. He doesn't speak to me in words. But when our eyes meet, his thoughts pass to me like an electric charge, forming messages in my mind.

I can feel his misery and frustration, though I assure him that the alternative would be worse. "By now you would be dead if you had been left to roam the wilds," I tell him. But that is of little consolation to either him or me. He should have been a prince, lord of his empire, no matter how brief his reign. Instead he is a prisoner.

I see him seldom now. I can do nothing for him.

I graduated into adolescence, enduring the afflictions of puberty—the acne, the lethargy and the rebelliousness. I graduated from high school and set off to explore the shores I had imagined had once been washed by the waves rolling in from Puget Sound.

I would be nearly 30 before I would come home once more to stay. The years of my odyssey into adulthood brought me back and forth across the United States several times. I basked in the South Seas sunshine and shivered through nights alive with the midnight sun. It was a turbulent journey, filled with wondrous innocence and cruel reality. Along the way, I matured as a woman and as a person.

The worst traumas of my physical evolution were all but over. My psychic evolution was about to begin.

It began in earnest on a Friday in 1959. I was driving from Aberdeen, Washington, to my home in Federal Way, a suburb south of Seattle. I was working as a sales representative for a major cosmetics firm and had just made my final call of the week. I enjoyed the work, especially on weeks like this one, when I had easily met my sales quota.

It was shortly after 4 p.m., as I sped along I-5 through Olympia, mentally rearranging my schedule to guarantee that I'd be ready in time for my date, who was picking me up at seven. Figuring it would take me another hour to reach Federal Way, I decided to postpone several errands until the next morning. That would leave plenty of time to transform myself from businesswoman into bombshell.

I barely noticed the tall, angular man hunched at the shoulder of a curving stretch of highway. Why should I? I had never picked up a hitchhiker in my life. And I have never since. Yet for some reason, I felt a compulsion to offer this one a lift. It was dangerous and foolish, I decided later, but I braked hard, then backed my car a quarter of a mile along the shoulder of the freeway.

As the stranger squeezed himself into the seat beside me, I began to tremble. "My gosh," I thought, "what a stupid thing to do."

"Don't be afraid, Shirlee," he said with a smile.

Had he read my thoughts, I wondered. How did he know my name? I drove nervously northward, watching him suspiciously out of the corner of my eye. I felt for my purse, which rested against my thigh, securely closed. He hadn't gotten my name off of anything inadvertently spilled from it. The car registration, I thought, glancing at the sun visor to which it was clipped. But the visor was still in the up position, concealing the registration card.

Yet instead of becoming frantic, my usual reaction in times of crisis, I felt myself drifting into euphoria, as if I'd just had a morphine injection. There was certainly nothing threatening about him, I decided.

There were, however, a lot of things odd about him. Though the day was very hot, he wore a heavy pin-striped suit with long-out-of-date wide lapels. The suit, accentuated by a wide-brimmed black hat he wore pulled low over his eyes, gave him the appearance of an extra from some ancient gangster film.

Despite his eerieness, I felt as if I had known him forever, a fact which set off new alarms in my conscious mind. Suddenly, he was telling me things about myself that I'd never told anyone.

Common sense demanded that I proceed with caution. I pulled off the interstate and parked at a drive-in restaurant, torn between hoping he'd thank me politely and look for another ride, and the urge to prolong this fascinating, if somewhat disturbing encounter.

I was still debating with myself about whether I wanted him to stay or go when he followed me into the restaurant. We found a table in the corner and I ordered coffee and an ice cream cone but was unsuccessful in persuading him to order something. "I'll buy," I blurted when I realized he may not have any money. He shook his head.

We waited in silence. Then, when my coffee and ice cream arrived, I impulsively shoved the cone into his hand. "Here, you take this," I commanded.

He studied the cone a long time before cautiously taking a lick. A delighted smile spread across his face as he attacked the ice cream voraciously. It was obvious this guy had never seen ice cream before.

I sipped my coffee slowly, pondering this gaunt stranger, wondering if the emotion I felt was pity or awe.

We spoke little as we climbed back into the car and headed north once more.

We were cruising through Tacoma before it dawned on me that I didn't know where he wanted out. "Oh, this'll be fine," he said, looking around with only vague interest.

"Take this," I said, handing him a ten-dollar bill as he climbed from the car. "And don't worry about repaying it. If you ever meet someone who needs it, just pass it along."

He smiled then and called goodbye as I pulled back into traffic. I glanced into the rear view mirror for a last glimpse of my gangling friend. He was gone.

I pulled off the road, looking frantically up and down the highway. There was nowhere for him to hide, yet he was nowhere to be seen. He had vanished. If he had existed at all.

I rummaged quickly through my purse, confirming that I was definitely $10 lighter than when I started out. Where had it gone if not to him? But if it had gone to him, where had he gone?

My family was on the verge of committing me to a padded room as I raved on about the man who had all but disappeared before my very eyes.

"It's probably the heat," my sister-in-law Edna suggested.

"Lie down and rest," my mother counseled.

"It was a hallucination," concluded my sister.

"But what about my $10?" I protested feebly.

I was lying down, resting when my sister-in-law called an hour later. She lived just a few miles away and after seeing that my mother's prescription of rest was being followed, had slipped out so she could be sure of getting home and fixing dinner before my hungry brother arrived there from work.

"Shirlee?" Edna said in a strained voice. "Come over here right away."

"I can't," I answered sarcastically, still irritated that she hadn't believed my story. "I'm resting."

"You must," she insisted, almost hysterically. Then the phone went dead.

I raced to my brother's house, sure I would find a raging fire or one of the children lying lifelessly on the floor. Instead, Edna was drinking coffee with one of her neighbors, a man I knew only as Everett.

At first, I was tempted to berate her about the damage a call like that could do to a person's circulatory system. Then I noticed Everett's face. It was as pale as the ash of the cigarette he raised to his lips with trembling hands.

Unconsciously I steadied myself against the kitchen table, then eased myself down onto a chair as Edna recounted Everett's story.

Everett traveled for a tire company and had just returned from a sales trip to Eastern Washington. He had been driving through the desert near Ephrata when he saw a man standing along the side of the road. I turned quizzically to Everett, who answered with a stunned nod. I knew the rest of the story already.

The country there is dry, hot and flat, so flat that you can see for miles in any direction. Since there wasn't much traffic on the highway, Everett had stopped to give the man a lift.

"Shirlee, that man knew my name before I said a word," Everett interrupted as Edna described the hitch-hiker's wardrobe—a dark pin-stiped suit, with a hat pulled down over his eyes.

"He must have sensed how uneasy I was because he

said, 'Don't be afraid, Everett.' But that just scared me more."

Everett had driven no more than a mile when the man suddenly asked to be let out. "Are you sure you want out here?" Everett protested as he pulled to the side of the highway.

"Yes, this will be fine," the stranger answered. The man walked toward the back of the car while Everett waivered uncertainly between caution and good samaritanism. "At first I was just going to drive on," Everett explained, but it was just too hot to leave him out there." Everett made up his mind to throw caution to the wind, but when he turned determinedly to urge the stranger back into the car, the stranger was gone.

By the time he arrived home, Everett had succeeded in convincing himself that he'd suffered a mild attack of rapture of the road, the hypnotic state that comes with too many uninterrupted miles of highway. Then his wife had related the story she'd heard from Edna, who'd apparently been spreading the news about Crazy Shirlee as she wended her way homeward.

We pondered the puzzle through two pots of coffee but it was obvious from the outset that it had no solution. I was late for my date which turned out to be a disaster since all I could think or talk about was the gaunt stranger.

How could anyone be at two different places separated by hundreds of miles at nearly the same time, I wondered aloud. No one seemed to have the answer, least of all me.

CHAPTER 2

The man of my dreams was not exactly the man of my dreams. He drifted into my unconscious gowned in flowing white robes. He led me on journeys to places that never existed—at least never in this world.

How can I describe his features? His face was a diaphanous pool, into which expressions merely sank away as new ones floated to the surface. His eyes were dark, angular slits that seemed to focus on nothing in particular but at the same time seemed to capture everything. His lips never moved, yet he spoke ceaselessly during our brief visits. I felt rather than read his emotions, I sensed rather than heard the answers to the myriad questions that raced through my mind.

Several years had passed since I had left the stranger at the edge of the highway, but I recognized him immediately the first time he came to me in my dreams. Gone were the out-of-date pin-striped suit and the fedora, but it was unmistakably the same man.

And now I knew his name. Xan.

I was living in a Seattle apartment house when I met another man, one of flesh and blood, who would soon become my husband.

At first I was hesitant about telling Gordon about my nocturnal visitor. But at last I decided that if we were going to share our lives together, I had better share this dark secret as well.

Gordon was incredulous. "You actually believe all

this is really happening?" he asked.

"I don't have much choice," I explained. I wasn't sure if he thought I was insane or was afraid he would somehow be dragged into my midnight meanderings.

"They are just dreams," he said, his tone wavering uncertainly between a question and a declaration.

"I'm not sure," I admitted. "But there are other things."

"Such as?"

I told him about the man in the orange flight suit.

I had been working for the Army, supervising a post exchange at Fort Lawton Army Base at the north end of Seattle when I was asked to temporarily expand my responsibilities to include the PX at Paine Field, an air force base 20 miles further north.

The man in the orange flight suit barged into my life one evening as I was leaving the Paine Field PX after an especially trying day. When I first saw him approaching along the sidewalk, I thought I recognized him as a man I had dated, a coast guard pilot. Odd, I thought, that Jim, who had recently been transferred to the East Coast, should show up at Paine Field wearing an air force flight suit and without warning me he was coming.

But when I looked into his face, I realized the man in the orange flight suit was not Jim. I smiled an apology for my rude stare and was about to brush past when he called me by name.

"Do I know you?" I asked hesitantly.

"Not yet," he answered, "But I'd certainly like to take you out tonight."

I was unattached at the time but I was not in the habit of going out with strangers. I declined demurely.

"Just dinner," he persisted. "You need a night out once in a while."

He was right about that. I had immersed myself in work. I enjoyed the challenge of the added responsibility and hadn't yet come to the realization that by working twice as hard for a lot more hours, I had effectively cut my pay in half. But I did realize that men named Jack aren't the only ones dulled by all work and no play.

I clung tenaciously to my resolve, however, warding off temptation with lame excuses.

The man in the orange flight suit was a worthy adversary, though. He countered with promises of sensual delight—a thick steak, soft music, dim lights, red wine. Then he delivered the coup de grace.

"I'm not on the make," he vowed. "Honest. Just dinner. That's all."

I've always resisted temptation but, unfortunately, I've seldom conquered it.

"All right," I acquiesced. "An early dinner and then I've got to get home. I've got to be up early."

We piled into my car and drove to nearby Mukilteo. Just my luck, I thought, to get stuck with a date with no transportation.

But dinner turned out to be quite pleasant. And the man in the orange flight suit turned out to be as good as his word. There were no passes.

Instead we chatted. I told him about myself and he smiled in all the right places. Then I listened as he explained that he was from Denver, that he had flown in that day to analyze base preparedness—how long it would take to transform it to combat efficiency in case of military attack.

Over brandy, he revealed his silver pin. "This is for you," he said, gently laying the finely engraved metal in my hand.

"I couldn't," I protested, gazing at what appeared to be a tiny model spacecraft perfect in detail yet no larger than a tie tack.

"It's an OGO," he said, ignoring my protest. "It's a memento that was given to everyone who worked on the project."

"OGO?"

"Orbiting Geophysical Observatory," he said. "The satellite."

"Oh," I nodded. I didn't even know what a geophysical observatory was, let alone that we had launched one into orbit around the earth seven months earlier. But I decided to keep OGO.

I dropped the man in the orange flight suit off at Paine Field about 9 p.m., and drove on south to my apartment in Seattle. I stared for a long time at OGO before I finally undressed for bed. I seldom wear jewelry—in fact, I don't even wear a wedding ring. But for some reason I pinned it to the dress I planned to wear the next day.

I was still in the shower the following morning when I heard a knock at the door. I quickly toweled off the excess water so I wouldn't drip all over the rug, then threw the towel around me and hurried to the door expecting to find one of the women who worked for me at the Fort Lawton Post Exchange.

I opened the door just a crack, just in case, and there stood the man in the orange flight suit. I felt anger and confusion boiling up within me. Here was a man with no car 20 miles from the base at which I had dropped him the night before. I had an unlisted phone number and no one—*but no one*—was allowed to give out my address. How had he found me? I felt betrayed.

"Don't be afraid, Shirlee," he said as he pushed the door open, then shoved me into the living room. Rape, I thought. Instead, he herded me to the wall, his arms outstretched above my head. I cowered before him as in that instant the floor began to tremble. Furniture rattled angrily, pictures swayed and glass throughout the apartment sang. Slowly it dawned on my that we were in the throes of an earthquake. That quake of April 29, 1965 would prove to be the worst to hit the Seattle area in recorded time, 6.5 on the Richter scale.

The man in the orange flight suit was protecting me. At first I didn't know whether to be offended or grateful. All I could think of was that rescue workers sifting through the rubble of my apartment would find my towel-clad body lying beneath a complete stranger in an orange flight suit and no one was ever going to believe it was all totally innocent.

The quake lasted mere seconds, but my panic-stricken brain gauged it at several hours. Then, slowly, the room grew quiet once more.

"You're going to be needed now," the man in the orange flight suit said simply.

I adjourned on wobbly legs to the privacy of my bedroom, where I dressed quickly. We drove to Fort Lawton where I checked out the post exchange. I was proud of my staff. Stock was already on the shelves and damaged items were laid out on the counter beneath a sign proclaiming, "Earthquake Sale."

I started to suggest that it didn't look like I was needed so badly after all. But like the Lone Ranger concluding another of his half-hour adventures, the man in the orange flight suit was gone.

I never saw him again, though I have wondered many times whether I misunderstood when he said I would be needed.

"My OGO?" was Gordon's response to the tale of the man in the orange flight suit.

OGO had become my trademark. I had worn it religiously in the months following the earthquake. It was the only jewelry I ever wore. But it was enough.

OGO was both admired and coveted. One man I dated had gone so far as to offer to buy it but I said no. Then I met Gordon. And on a whim, before we had even discussed marriage, I gave it to him one evening. But I neglected to tell him its history.

Gordon seemed momentarily crestfallen. "My OGO?" he repeated. Then he composed himself.

"And you expect me to believe that story?" he asked.

I shrugged noncommittally. But apparently he did believe me or was at least willing to accept me with all my faults and aberrations, including what were obviously extraordinary flights of fancy. Plans for the wedding proceeded.

Then one day several weeks before the wedding, Gordon surprised me by announcing that he could accept my fantasies as fact if he had a sign, something to indicate that there was a thread of reality in the tales I had woven for him. He didn't exactly establish the sign as a condition for our marriage but it sure sounded like one.

That night, just before falling asleep, I concentrated on Xan. I had never before summoned him to my dreams and I wasn't sure I could, but Xan appeared on cue.

When I told him my problem, Xan just stared at me for a long time. "So Mr. Krehnke wants a sign," he said at last, irritation in the voice that came to me telepathically. All right then, he'll have his sign."

I told Gordon the next day that Xan would grant his wish, he would have his sign. Then we waited. But the sign didn't come.

Fortunately, though, we had other things on our minds as we frantically prepared for the wedding. Not only did we have to plan for a swarm of out-of-town guests but before the Saturday ceremony, we hoped to be moved into a house we had bought near my parents' home in Federal Way.

For security reasons, neither Gordon nor anyone below the senior officers of the computer firm for which he worked had keys to his office. So when he left for home the Thursday before our wedding, he loaded up his briefcase with several urgent files.

He planned on squeezing his homework into our honeymoon if he had time. I was determined that he would have neither the time nor the inclination. But first I had to survive the chaos before the calm.

We spent Friday juggling half-packed moving boxes and future in-laws I'd never met. In cars stuffed like the cheeks of a ravenous hamster, we chugged to Federal Way, where we hurled cartons through the front door of our romantic bungalow, then raced back to the airport just in time to meet the next arrivals.

I don't think Gordon's family ever got over its first

impression of me, my hair a hydra of disjointed curls, my face unmarred by make-up, my clothes a perfect wardrobe for a CARE commercial. A vision of loveliness I was not. Neither was Gordon. But then he didn't have to be. He was theirs.

By midnight Friday it was obvious we weren't going to make it into our new house by the wedding. We surrendered to fatigue and the fates.

Saturday morning found Gordon unpacking boxes at his apartment as rapidly as he'd been packing them the day before. First he couldn't find his razor. Then his socks were missing. In the process of putting himself together, he all but dismantled the living room. Books lay strewn across the floor. An army of cologne bottles stood attentively on an end table. From the middle of the couch rose a mountain of unironed clothes.

And atop the mountain of clothes sat Gordon's brother from Nebraska, watching Gordon fidget and pace, pausing every several seconds to ask what time it was.

"You got a cigarette?" Gordon the non-smoker asked, perhaps as much to change the subject as to relieve his jitters. His brother tapped one from his pack, then handed Gordon a lighter embossed with the crest of a religious fraternity unique to Nebraska.

Gordon lost track of the lighter after that. When his brother asked for it following the wedding ceremony, Gordon rifled the pockets of his suit. "I thought I gave it back," he concluded sheepishly.

"No," his brother answered shortly, irritation in his voice.

"Well, never mind," Gordon assured him, "it's got to be back at the apartment." But it wasn't.

"We'll find it when we unpack," Gordon announced with mock-confidence. "I'll send it to you."

On Tuesday, Gordon left me with a houseful of unpacked boxes and headed back to the work-a-day world. I was proud of the fact that he'd only had time to glance at his homework last Monday night.

"See if you can find the lighter," he said, giving me a peck on the lips and a pat on the behind on his way out the door.

An hour later, he called. "Allright," he said, his voice noticeably shaky, "you win."

"I got the sign," he answered.

Gordon had been at his desk, examining the files he'd brought along on our honeymoon when he realized that several important documents were missing. "Where are they?" he had asked his secretary, who speculated they might be in the "bastard" file, a drawer in an extra desk kept under lock and key at the other end of the building.

With the key she'd given him, he unlocked the desk and found the documents. Then, he had opened the middle drawer in search of a paper clip. And there he found it. Not the paper clip he had expected but his brother's cigarette lighter.

Xan, I decided, has a warped sense of humor.

Strange things now began occurring with alarming regularity.

As we struck up acquaintances with our new neighbors, most of them families of air traffic controllers for the FAA, we began to hear strange tales. Such as the story of the UFO they swore they'd seen on a clear night the year before but which the Air Force totally discounted. Or the strange man in the pin-striped suit at least five neighbors saw walk down the street one sunny morning only to disappear before their eyes.

The hair on my arms stood up as if alive with static electricity.

Gordon and I had been in our house several months when I took my first trip to Las Vegas. And at no time did my head leave the pillow. Xan took me.

He was very good about taking me places. The only problem was that when we got where we were going, I had no idea where we were and when I got back home, I had no idea where I had been. He had a knack for leading me on tours of places I couldn't find on any map and showing me things I didn't understand.

Take for instance the night we passed through time and space into an amphitheater surrounded by grassy knolls. Seated on these knolls were an assortment of creatures straight out of your worst nightmare. Yet for some reason, I felt neither terror nor revulsion. Instead, I willingly joined them on the knoll absorbing knowledge from some unseen source.

Another time we visited a room filled with what can best be described as chairs. These were arranged in semi-circular rows facing a wall divided into three screens. From this room, Xan explained, it is possible to scan any area one wished, merely by willing it. And with that the screens lit up with a view of a barren landscape which quickly dissolved into a verdant rain forest.

It was all terribly fascinating.

But for once, I wanted to go someplace that would stimulate my senses rather than just arouse my curiosity. Someplace like Las Vegas. I've always been attracted to glitter.

"I think I'll go to Las Vegas," I announced one night as Gordon sat reading the newspaper after dinner.

"Mmmhmmm," he answered.

"Tonight," I added.

He looked over the edge of the newspaper as if at an incorrigible child. But he said nothing more.

"I never ask Xan for much," I pouted. "I figure he can do one little favor for me, just this once."

Gordon returned to his newspaper.

In bed that night, I concentrated. I envisioned the dress I would wear, a tight fitting black job that showed off lots of cleavage. And as I dozed off, I thought about Xan and about pictures I had seen of the nightlife in the Vegas casinos. As I dreamed, I was there, gowned in the dress I had ordered, drifting among throngs ponying up to the slot machines and bending intently over the gaming tables.

Next day, I described the dream to Gordon, who

popped my balloon by allowing as how he sometimes willed his own dreams by concentrating on some fantasy just before falling asleep. He went off on some long-winded story about an overinflated blonde who used to occupy his fantasies when he was in college.

Then, several days later, I heard the phone ring. Gordon answered it. "She's never been to Las Vegas," he said. He listened a moment longer, then hung up the phone.

"Who was that?" I asked.

"Caroline," he answered peevishly. "Wanted to know how you liked Vegas."

I raced to the phone. "Caroline," I shouted when she answered, "What about Las Vegas?"

"I'm sorry, Shirlee," Caroline apologized, "I didn't mean to cause any trouble."

Poor dear. Caroline thought that my marriage must already be on the rocks, married less than six months and I was already stepping out on Gordon.

"It's all right," I assured her. "Tell me about Las Vegas."

Caroline laid out an eerie tale about how our mutual friend Sybil had just returned from a week there and how one night in the casino she had seen me across the room, standing alone, watching the players. She described my gown in detail, a tight-fitting black crepe with a low neckline. Sybil had waved and started toward me but just then I had been paged over the loudspeaker and had headed off apparently in search of a house phone. She hadn't seen me again.

Caroline went silent as I began to laugh dementedly. "It was just a dream," I explained at last. Caroline listened as I described how I happened to be in Las Vegas that night.

"Sometimes you worry me," she said at last.

Gordon was more emphatic. "Shirlee, you've got to stop this," he said when I told him Sybil had seen me in a Las Vegas casino.

My smile of triumph faded. "I'll try," I said, crestfallen.

I did try. Honestly, I did. But then I met Eunice.

A woman's heartbroken sobs awoke me from a deep sleep. I lay still a moment, listening. All I could hear was Gordon snoring softly beside me. I nudged him awake. "Whazzamatter?" he mumbled.

"Listen," I whispered, "there's somebody in the house." He too heard the sobbing and now it was joined by the sound of someone pacing in another part of our house.

We quietly climbed out of bed. I huddled close behind Gordon as he eased open the door to the recreation room. We gazed into the dimly lit room. There was no one there.

A foul, overpowering odor swept suddenly through the half-open door.

Almost gagging, we stumbled through the recreation room into the living room. Moonlight filtered through the leaves of a giant old maple tree on the front lawn, casting crazy patterns on the walls. But there seemed to be no one but Gordon and me in the house.

We turned on the lights and searched every nook and cranny. By now, even the awful smell had evaporated.

"It's a ghost," I said.

"Naw," Gordon yawned as he settled back in bed. "Just a dream. . . ."

"We both had the same dream?" I countered, but he was already past caring, bound up in the warm sheets, cradled in the warm arms of slumber.

The same thing happened the next night. And the next. And the next.

Every night we were awakened by sounds of sobbing and pacing. And every night the dreadful septic smell permeated the house.

Gordon had our sewer lines checked but there was nothing wrong with them. Even Gordon was beginning to wonder if the house was haunted but we tried to shrug the whole thing off.

Ours was hardly the stereotypical haunted house. It

was a modern three-bedroom rambler in an unpretentious neighborhood. Nothing about it suggested it came equipped with a spirit—no creaking stairs, no shadowy cellar, not even a cobweb-shrouded attic.

As if determined to prove that a ghost doesn't need a house with seven gables to do its haunting, Eunice started playing rough.

I was sipping coffee, talking to my sister on the telephone when Gordon appeared one morning at the kitchen doorway, a favorite necktie in his hands. It was in tatters.

"Look what those damn cats did," he complained, an annoyed look on his face. Our cats were playful and mischievous but they'd never before been destructive. Gordon angrily finished dressing for work, went to the den for his briefcase, then kissed me goodbye and left for the office.

I talked on the phone a few more minutes, poured myself a second cup of coffee and headed for the bedroom. Entering the recreation room on the way, I almost fainted. The room was a shambles. Books were strewn all over. Pillows, decorative dishes and clothes were tossed about. And Gordon's now-knotted tie lay on top of the mess.

I have never been a *House Beautiful* housekeeper but the room had been reasonably neat when I had passed through it on my way to the kitchen that morning. Someone must have broken in while I was on the phone, I thought. Anxiously, I checked the doors and windows, afraid the culprit might still be lurking about. But the doors were locked and the windows showed no sign of entry.

My hands shook as I dialed Gordon's office. He wasn't in yet, but his secretary gave him my near-hysterical message. He rushed home to find me still standing in the middle of the ravaged room.

He turned pale when he spotted the necktie. "I threw that in the wastebasket in the den," he said. The den was on the far side of the house, with the kitchen and living room between it and the recreation room. No one could have walked through without me seeing them.

We sat on the sofa, completely bewildered. As we talked, Gordon tried to unknot the tie but the knots were too tightly drawn for him to make any headway. Then, a favorite milk-glass dish which had been hanging on the wall suddenly came hurtling across the room, smashing on the wall behind my head.

Terrified, we fled to the kitchen. We waited there a long time but nothing more happened.

That night, however, the sobbing and pacing resumed.

The strain was beginning to show on both Gordon and me. We moved cautiously through the house when we were alone. When together, we preferred the buddy system, ambling like Siamese twins on the endless errands that fill the hours of homelife.

Perhaps dinner guests would prove a healthy diversion. The invitation to Pete, a friend of Gordon's, and his wife had been issued some time past, but I'm sure neither realized that we were looking forward to their visit for more than just social reasons.

We were drinking coffee in the living room after dinner when Pete asked me to tell his wife some of the weird things Gordon had been describing having happened in the house. I was embarrassed and told him I'd rather not.

Suddenly, the lights in the room began blinking. A swag lamp over the sofa where our guests were sitting began to swing violently from side to side.

"Shirlee," Pete's wife said as she rose quickly from the sofa, dodging the lamp in the process, "I enjoyed meeting you and dinner was delicious. But we're getting the hell out of here."

Gordon and I didn't know whether to laugh or cry. As the days wore on, we merely adapted. We were becoming accustomed to the other one in the house. It was a bit like having a new baby. We even learned to endure the midnight sobbing and pacing. Only the uncertainty of the periodic violent outbursts continued to haunt us.

Then one hot afternoon the following summer, I met our ghost.

I had prepared lunch for 12 women from the neighborhood and someone had brought along an ouija board for entertainment.

Two of my friends began asking questions like: "Am I going to be rich?" But the pointer kept jumping to the letter "S". Jokingly, one of the women said: "Gee, Shirlee, maybe it wants to talk to you."

With that, the pointer leaped to "Yes."

"Come on," I answered incredulously, "I don't believe in ouija boards." And with that, the curtains over my kitchen window burst into flames. I jerked the curtains from the rod and threw them into the sink, where I flooded them with tap water. I searched for some organic reason for the fire, knowing full well I would find none. The stove was on the other side of the kitchen and it hadn't even been turned on that day. There was no earthly cause for the fire.

I decided I'd better talk to the board.

Feeling like a fool, I rested my hands on the pointer. "Are you the ghost that's running around my house?" I asked.

The board rapidly spelled out "MY HOUSE." A chill settled over everyone in the room.

The pointer started shaking then. And so did I. I couldn't take my hands off it.

At that moment, Gordon came in. He saw what was happening and knocked the board away. "Okay, Shirlee," he said, "this has gone far enough. We're going to get to the bottom of it."

Gordon was a computer expert, a no nonsense pragmatist who found it all but impossible to accept the occult. There had to be an explanation and he was determined to find it.

While an army of experts poured over the house in search of faults or defects that could explain these strange phenomena, Gordon began sifting through the house's history. The experts came up empty-handed but Gordon made some unnerving discoveries.

A couple named Eunice and Ed had built the house 15 years earlier, he was told. They had one child, a boy known throughout the neighborhood simply as TNT. TNT, according to those who remembered, was the apple of his mother's eye, though he wasn't as highly regarded by the neighbors, who characterized him as spoiled and troublesome.

Ed's business had been on the verge of bankruptcy when he and Eunice decided on a "vacation" in California, where they could scout out the options open to them. They withdrew their savings from the bank to insure against creditors freezing their assets during their absence, then loaded up the car, placing a box filled with money under the front seat. The day before they left, Eunice confided in a neighbor about the money, "just in case."

Perhaps she had a premonition of disaster. If so, it proved accurate.

The car was involved in a head-on crash in California. Ed died instantly. Eunice died before she could be taken to a hospital. Miraculously, TNT survived unhurt, though neighbors lost track of him in the shuffle. Someone had heard he'd been taken in by relatives but no one knew for sure.

The house had been tied up in litigation for several years. Renters had come and gone in rapid succession until eventually the estate was settled. We had bought the house a short time later.

We called former renters we could track down to find out if they'd had any peculiar experiences. One woman described feeling cold in the house and said she had sensed that she was not alone. But she had never experienced anything like what we had been through.

At least now we thought we had some idea of the identity of our ghost. Eunice had apparently come back, perhaps in search of her lost child.

But instead of relieving our anxiety, the revelation only added to it.

Gordon and I were making arrangements to adopt a baby boy. What if Eunice resented the child's intrusion into the home, or worse yet, what if she adopted it as the reincarnation of TNT?

We had a lonely, confused spirit and a house to de-haunt. But we hadn't the faintest idea how to go about it.

As if we didn't have enough problems, exorcists began showing up uninvited with guarantees that they could put poor Eunice out of her misery once and for all. One sprinkled salt around the house. Another told me to walk around with a broom in my hands. And still another suggested that I sleep with the broom upside down on the bed.

Instead, I began reading everything I could find on the subject, finally settling on a volume by Hans Holsner, *Ghosts I Have Known*, which afforded what seemed a reasonable prescription.

Whenever we heard her sobbing, Gordon and I would recite religiously: "Eunice, you are dead. Go in peace." Then we'd say a prayer for her and reassure her that her boy was alive and well.

We felt like idiots but we persisted. And at last, Eunice came no more.

It was over, we assured one another. But in the back of my mind was lingering doubt that Eunice was gone forever. I was sure she would be back, that her spirit would never really escape the house.

But even more disturbing was the recurring fear that somehow I, too, had become irrevocably bound to our honeymoon bungalow.

CHAPTER 3

When Seattle's economy took off in the early 1960s, Gordon and I went along for the ride.

We launched our own business, a computer consulting firm. I was a corporate officer but all I really had to do was sit back and watch Gordon do the dirty work, which consisted primarily of hauling money to the bank. It really wasn't all that dirty, at least it didn't seem so at the time. Boeing Industries was making a killing in the airplane market and Boeing—combined with the U.S. government through a complex, entangling network of contracts—represented our largest single client; we were fast becoming rich.

Never mind that our prosperity was tied in part to a devastating undeclared war in Vietnam. For some reason, I never made the connection. Even if I had, I doubt that it would have troubled me. I had grown up with war, first in Europe and the Pacific, later in Korea. It seemed the natural order of things that some men died and others prospered.

We prospered. We traded in our honeymoon cottage for a mansion. I'd have followed Gordon into a cave, but I was much happier with the alternative.

The Spanish-style villa had been built in 1920 by a man who had founded the telephone company serving much of Washington's Olympic Peninsula. The lawn consisted of five acres of gardens, adjoining 25 acres of natural woodland. But the house itself was my pride and joy. Its living room alone was nearly as large as the bungalow we had left behind.

It always amused me that Eunice's spirit would dwell in that mundane little house, while the villa, which looked like the classic haunted castle, never had a ghost to its name.

The only thing eerie about the house was its capacity for devouring large sums of money for remodeling and updating. We spent $10,000 on the kitchen alone, but never figured out how to wire it so we could operate the furnace and a multitude of modern appliances simultaneously.

Gordon and I never begrudged having to spend the money, though. We were lucky to get the house at all. And we got it at a bargain price.

We bought it from a woman whose husband had died young, leaving her with four small children and a modest life insurance policy. She had merged the insurance money and an uncanny business sense to produce a fortune in real estate transactions.

She had bought the villa, including the original furnishings, to use as a beach house while the children were still small enough to enjoy the water. But as they grew up and moved away, she had lost interest in the magnificent old house.

Lake Bay was a prosperous Puget Sound community that boasted a surplus of families wealthy enough to make sizeable offers on the house they called The Castle. But the now-old woman had politely declined.

For some reason, though, she took a liking to Gordon and me. Perhaps we reminded her of her own lost youth.

A mutual friend arranged for us to visit the house one Sunday afternoon. Gordon and I were awestruck. It's the house I always dreamed about, I told Gordon, though in fact I didn't think I had ever had such ambitious dreams.

"Let's make her an offer," Gordon suggested.

We spent the evening hunched over our bankbook. It

didn't look good. But next day we drove to the old woman's apartment over a department store she owned in Port Orchard. The building didn't look like much from the outside, but the apartment was large and comfortable, reflecting with quiet dignity the great wealth this woman possessed.

Gordon got quickly to the point, turning our casual conversation to the house on Lake Bay. "Would you consider selling it?" he asked, his face red with tension.

The old woman didn't answer. Instead, she poured tea.

Gordon swallowed. "All we can afford is $50,000," he apologized.

She dabbed at the corners of her mouth with a prim white napkin.

"It is a beautiful home," I interjected, hoping to save Gordon any more embarrassment. "I can see why it would be hard to part with." But still she avoided the issue.

Nothing more was said on the subject of the Lake Bay villa. We chatted about our mutual friend's health and thanked the old woman for allowing us the opportunity to see her beach house firsthand. After a polite interval, we exchanged goodbyes, and Gordon and I headed forlornly back to our bungalow in Federal Way.

But a few days later, Gordon got a call from the old woman's attorney. "Mrs. Cortney accepts your offer," he said with formality. "But you will have to take over the property as is—with the furniture that's in there and without any repairs."

Less formally he added, "Christ, did you get a deal!"

I cried as Gordon and I toured that great mansion in the dwindling light of our first evening there. Our seven-month-old son Jason was asleep on the second floor.

We began in the foyer, pretending we were guests here in the house for the first time.

Wrought iron doors inlaid with Eisenglass opened into the living room, where a trio of couches held court among clusters of stuffed chairs scattered the length of the narrow room. A week before, hazy clouds had wafted toward the vaulted ceiling rising to cathedral height above us as the ancient dust covers were pulled off and the cleaning begun. Now, everything was spotless.

I leaned against the concert piano, watching Gordon fiddle with his new stereo far away at the other end of the room. I felt as though I were in the lobby of a very expensive hotel.

Three French doors opened from the living room to a covered patio extending the length of the house. We stood on the patio a moment listening to waves lap gently at the beach before us. We strolled through another set of French doors into the formal dining room.

The giant oak table stretched nearly 15 feet down the center of the room leaving space for a huge buffet at one end. To the right was the kitchen, which still needed work. But it had promise.

Adjacent to the kitchen was the maid's quarters, sparse but comfortable.

Also on the first floor was the library, the master bedroom and bath. Upstairs were two more bedrooms and another bath.

God, I felt decadent. And I loved it. I'll take wretched excess to impoverished distress any day.

"Won't you get bored?" one of my friends asked when she found out I had quit my job to devote full time to my life of leisure.

I couldn't help laughing.

From experience, I can attest that being out of work is delightful, as long as you can afford it. I never lifted a finger around the house and I have never been happier.

We had a one-armed gardener named Owen who kept the grounds as immaculate as the maid kept the house. Neither of them lived with us, though. The maid's quarters were occupied by the live-in "nurse" who cared for Jason.

I kept myself busy with various civic organizations, socializing with friends and planning lavish dinner parties. Periodically, though, I suffered bouts of anxiety, the poor-little-rich-girl syndrome. It just wasn't natural to be so happy. Something had to go wrong.

But the cure for such anxiety was simple. I'd lie down on our plush, king-size bed and roll myself up in the satin sheets and in a while the depression would pass.

Gordon smiled indulgently when I broke the news that Xan had made the transition with us. Gordon had learned to accept my aberration with good-natured chagrin and was even willing to listen to Xan's counsel on business affairs. In fact, it had been Xan who came up with the idea of our getting into business for ourselves.

I think Gordon even forgave Xan for conspiring with me to suddenly extend our family without consulting with him. It occurred shortly after we moved into the villa. Xan had once more invaded my dreams, once more gesturing for me to follow.

I lifted myself from my sleeping body and floated with him to a doomed city which was as real to me as the room I had left behind. Outside the doom was a feeling of turmoil but as we passed through into the city itself, I was filled with calm.

As we ascended, I could see there were no cars or other visible machinery of any kind. Muted voices drifted up to us as what appeared to be conveyor belts whisked human forms along what would otherwise be sidewalks.

We settled on one of these conveyors and Xan began pushing buttons on a box attached to his belt. Then he stood back and watched as we glided through canyons between towering structures of unusual geometric shape.

We toured the city for what seemed like hours before the conveyor finally stopped before a large building whose tiny windows were covered with metal screens. As I gazed inside. I saw a wizened old man behind a desk, running his hands over a book whose pages I could not see.

"What is he doing?" The question formed in my mind but was never spoken.

"He reads through his fingers," Xan answered telepathically.

"What is he reading?"

"He is The Keeper," Xan answered, as though by that I should comprehend.

"Keeper of what?"

"Of souls—those are the records of souls."

I studied the walls of the room. They were lined with large file drawers, each with a small round window. Inside, I realized, were babies yet to be born.

"These are special children," Xan told me. "They will be born with unique gifts. Soon, many will arrive on earth, bringing knowledge and wisdom to help your troubled world."

But each child must await the proper vehicle and the proper moment before it could be born, he added, as I focused on a shock of red hair visible through one tiny window.

"Is that a girl?" I asked.

"I cannot say," he answered, following my gaze.

"If it is, may I have her?"

"I cannot say," he answered once more.

Apparently, I was getting a little too pushy. The dream was over, if, indeed, it was a dream.

Next morning, I thought about the red-haired baby. Like most women, I longed for a daughter to dress in frills and fancy dresses, to give the things I had wished for as a child. I put the dream in the back of my mind and thought no more about it.

Several weeks passed when I received a call from a woman at the agency through which we had adopted Jason. At first I assumed it was a routine follow-up call, just to make sure everything was going smoothly.

But tension in the woman's voice alarmed me. Surely they don't repossess babies, I thought. Jason was fine

and we were all very busy, I said, hoping for an abrupt
end to the conversation.

"Shirlee," she interrupted, "we've had another birth
and it's astrologically perfect for you—Aquarius."

Now, I was really alarmed. What made her think I
believe in astrology? I did, but what made her think so?
These people can be awfully forward, I thought.

"No," I told her, "one baby at a time is plenty. We
don't want another one. Not right now, anyway."

But during the ensuing lull in the conversation, my
curiosity got the better of me. "What is it," I asked, "a
girl?"

"Well . . . ." She dragged her answer out too long to
have much of a tranquilizing effect.

"We've already got a boy," I exclaimed.

"It's twins," she admitted softly.

"Oh, God," I shrieked. "Twins! No, no, no, I can't
take twins."

"Shirlee, we can't find a home for both of them, and if
you won't take them, we'll have to split them up."

I'm nothing if not a rock in times of distress.
"Okay," I heard myself say, "I'll take them." Sight
unseen, without even consulting with Gordon, I had
committed us to raising two more children.

How could I have done something so stupid, I wondered. But they were going to split them up like a litter
of puppies, I reasoned. The recriminations and ration-
alizations raged on within me throughout the remainder of the morning.

Finally, Gordon called. The moment of truth had
come. Better to break the news over the phone, I figured, mustering the sweetest voice in my arsenal. "I
have a little surprise for you, dear," I began. Did I ever.

Gordon waited patiently while I composed my
thoughts. "I got twins." I blurted it out, afraid that if I
hesitated even a moment, I would lose my courage.

"Twin what?" he asked.

"They were going to break up the set," I babbled.
"They'd be no trouble at all and please couldn't I keep

them?"

"Are you crazy?" he demanded. But there was a tone to his voice like the ring of fine china. Gordon could never deny me anything. And I think he was secretly delighted by the prospect of being a father once more.

"Happy Mother's Day," he sighed in mock exasperation.

The day the babies were to be delivered, Gordon teased me about needing a better method of birth control, then suggested that I be more careful next time I had the urge to place an order with Xan. Gordon had remembered.

We both had a shock when the babies finally arrived. The little girl had the brightest red hair that never came out of a Clairol bottle. And the bottoms of her tiny feet were grooved with lines forming a near-perfect X.

We named her Xanthea.

Her auburn-haired brother we named Nicholas.

The nurse now had plenty to keep her busy. She asked for more money and we gave it to her.

But the family wasn't done growing yet. I brought home an all-white boxer pup which was about to be put to sleep for no greater sin than no one else would take him. We named him Argos.

Then a friend brought us an orphaned fawn. I knew it was illegal to keep her but I couldn't think what else to do. We called her Delilah and she slept at the foot of our bed.

We must have seemed the idyllic American family when on sunny Sunday afternoons our little caravan wound its way down the road to the marina for an ice cream cone. Gordon led with Jason on his shoulders. Next came me with a twin in each arm. Following behind were the gangly fawn and the lumbering boxer Argos. We usually invited the nurse to join us but for some reason, she always declined.

Delilah spend her days gamboling through the gardens, much to Owen's dismay. The first time I heard our one-armed gardener shouting at the top of his lungs

and looked out to see him chasing Delilah around the
yard with the hoe, I intervened.

"What's the matter, Owen?"

"She eats the plants faster'n I can plant 'em," he
sputtered.

"Just shoo her away and plant some more," I counseled.

When he came to me in exasperation a week later and
announced that either Delilah went or he did, I explained that if that was the only alternative, I would
write him a check. But before he left, I suggested that he
consider the fact that he wasn't being paid at a piece
rate. No one was going to cut his salary if some of the
plants didn't survive.

Mumbling to himself, Owen trudged back toward the
gardens, waving angrily at Delilah who had been
watching through the window like a guilty child. Owen
decided to stay on as long as he didn't get the blame for
the shabby condition of the gardens.

When Delilah got so big that we were afraid she
might bolt through our bedroom window, or worse yet,
have a nightmare and slash Gordon and I to ribbons
with her jagged hooves, we evicted her from our bed. We
turned her out but she never strayed far from home, a
fact which continued to infuriate Owen and has haunted
me to this day.

Delilah had developed a taste for liquor. Whenever
we gathered with guests on the patio for drinks, Delilah
would saunter up and nonchalantly steal fruit out of
the sweet drinks. She was especially fond of cherries
and pineapple. But soon, she began showing a marked
preference for the alcohol. Somewhere along the line,
she became addicted to dry martinis—without olives.

At first, it was humorous to see her lapping content-
edly at the clear liquor. But as I began to consider the
potential consequences, I proclaimed that there would
be no more deer served at my house.

We were entertaining a large group of friends and
business acquaintances one warm spring night when

several guests strolled out onto the patio with drinks in hand. I should have been more alert. I should have warned them against sharing with Delilah. But I didn't think to.

From all reports, Delilah was soon guzzling martinis like a Madison Avenue ad executive, much to the delight of a guest who took it upon himself to be sure her thirst was adequately quenched. At last, she staggered off into the darkness.

We found her next morning at the bottom of a ravine where she had apparently tumbled in her drunken stupor. Her neck was broken. Delilah was dead.

I was furious. An otherwise intelligent man had thoughtlessly fed Delilah liquor, enough to get her falling down drunk. Then I remembered how tickled I had been the first time I saw her wobble away from the patio.

What is there about humans, I wonder, that compels us to share our vices with the rest of nature? The Humane Society is a fairly recent innovation. Until a century ago, the torture of animals solely for the pleasure of man was common throughout the Christian world. It still isn't unusual in some places.

How could I be so sanctimonious when I was not above reproach? I never said anything to the guest who had thoughtlessly given Delilah too much to drink. In fact, I never spoke to him again as long as he lived.

Though I would never forget Delilah, the pall that fell over the house with her death soon passed in a flurry of activity. The living room that had once reminded me of the lobby of a grand hotel now began to look more like Grand Central Station.

Every Saturday, we served sit-down dinner to at least a dozen guests—once we entertained 150 at a buffet. And there were often two more parties during the week.

It was good for business, Gordon and I reasoned, and it was good for us as well. We enjoyed the sparkle.

Even when there wasn't a party, we had guests. At all hours of the day and night, we would see strangers

strolling the gardens, admiring the man-made water-
fall, the perfectly manicured lawn and the beautifully-
maintained flower beds.

They would moor their boats at the marina a few
blocks away, then stride purposefully through the
"park," before presenting themselves sheepishly at our
door.

They had been admiring the house for years, they
would explain, and would we mind terribly if they took
a quick tour. We seldom refused.

Despite all the strangers milling about, I never worried over the children, even when they played outdoors.
Argos was by now full-grown and very protective. No
one except the immediate family dared touch them
when he was around.

But strangers weren't the only potential hazard
Argos was good at protecting them from. There was
water on two sides of the house, woods on the third and
beyond the gardens, a highway. The children never got
in harm's way, though. Argos never let them. Every
time one ventured too near what Argos considered
danger, he would intercede, herding an often outraged
toddler back to safety.

Sometimes we let the children stay up past bedtime
on party nights so guests could enjoy the spectacle of
their romps across the lawn beneath the watchful eye
of Argos. Eventually, though the children would be put
to bed, Argos would be rewarded with fresh, lean meat
and I would take over the chores of entertaining.

But entertaining was never a chore. I gloried in it. I
relished the act of slipping into something slinky and
reveled in the backslapping bawdiness of successful
men and the demure ribaldry of their beautiful women.

Then a strange thing began to occur with alarming
regularity. I have seldom been at a loss for words, but
suddenly I discovered that after a few drinks, I was
saying things without thinking them. The words were
somehow not my own.

I would brush against a well-tailored executive and

suddenly find myself talking to him about a business trip he had taken the week before or discreetly suggesting to his wife that the paperboy with the too tight Levis was far too young and far too dangerous.

Soon everyone who had been warned to be careful what they were thinking around me was asking me to try to read his thoughts. It became like a parlor game, a magic trick to amuse our guests.

I couldn't do it with everyone, though. Often, I would concentrate a long time and still be unable to come up with the thoughts of a person right next to me, then find myself tuning into someone on the other side of the room.

It is impossible to describe how these images came to me or the sensation of having someone else's thoughts filtering into my mind. It really has no parallel I can think of. Perhaps the closest I can come is to liken it to a memory that has lain dormant in the subconscious for years, only to surface suddenly for no apparent reason. Like a tune you don't recall ever having heard but which you suddenly find yourself humming.

"You'd better be damn careful what you say," Gordon warned sternly. He had noticed that I could only perform the stunt after several drinks. Perhaps it took the drinks to break down my inhibitions. But Gordon was concerned the drinks might break down too many inhibitions for my own good.

"Don't worry," I assured him with a laugh. "I know my limits."

I never worried about overstepping the bounds of good taste. I discovered that I'm an exhibitionist at heart. I thrived on all the attention I was getting. I enjoyed being risque. Periodically, I even tested myself by weaving perilously close to the edge of propriety. But I always knew when to veer away. I did know my limits.

Besides, I had other more pressing worries than whether I inadvertently offended a potential customer.

At the age of two, Xanthea had become a pyromaniac. Or so it seemed.

It had begun innocently enough. The maid tapped on our bedroom door one morning and softly asked Gordon and me to come with her. She led us into the kitchen and there on the floor before the refrigerator was Xanthea, sound asleep.

I picked her up and carried her to bed, then joined Gordon and Mully in the kitchen to see if we could puzzle out what Xanthea had been doing there. By the time I got back, Gordon had discovered cool air flowing from beneath the refrigerator, air being circulated by fans within the machine.

"She's probably too hot," Gordon suggested.

That sounded reasonable. I bought lighter pajamas for Xanthea. But next morning, and for several mornings more, we found her soundly sleeping at the foot of the refrigerator.

When we quizzed her on it, Xanthea couldn't explain why she was there or how she'd gotten to the kitchen.

We decided to close her bedroom door at night to see if that would solve the problem. It seemed to work. Xanthea wasn't in the kitchen the next morning.

But that night, I arose from bed after one of our parties and stumbled through the dark house, up the stairs toward Xanthia's bedroom. I don't know what force drew me. I was barely awake at the time. Maybe it was nothing more than a mother's intuition.

I leaned against her door, listening, but all was silence within. Slowly, I turned the knob and pushed it open. The room was filled with a strange glow that cast queer shadows on the walls. When I spotted the source of the light, I stood momentarily transfixed, watching flames dance around my sleeping child. The mattress was on fire.

But there was no smoke in the room.

I let out a shriek and raced to the bed, scooping Xanthea up in one arm, tossing her bed clothes over the flames with my free hand. I could hear Gordon stumbling dazedly up the stairs as I pounded at the flames.

Xanthea was awake now, crying in my arms. In the

next room, I could hear Jason and Nicholas coming to consciousness, calling out with frightened voices for Gordon and me. Gordon burst into the room, took Xanthea from my arms, started to back away, then returned the baby to me and began pounding on the blanket.

We searched a long time for matches but never found any. Nor did we find matches after several more incidents of mysterious fires.

I spent my nights in the darkness outside Xanthea's bedroom and catnapped during the day when the nurse could keep an eye on her.

But the tension was beginning to wear on me. I wasn't concerned so much about being consumed by flames as I was about losing Xanthea, my precious red-haired baby.

"You'd better see a doctor," Gordon said one morning as he watched me shuffle near exhaustion into our bedroom. "You look terrible."

I nodded noncommittally. But later that day, I called a physician, a personal friend, who told me to come right in. I explained that I thought I needed some sort of tranquilizer. I told him about my all-night vigils and their effect on me.

"It sounds like Xanthea needs a doctor worse than you," he replied.

I stared at him in shock.

"Look," he said, "pyromania is a sickness. I don't think it's very common with children that young but then again, I'm not a psychiatrist. Let me see if I can get you an appointment with one right away."

And without waiting for my consent, he picked up the telephone. I listened to his end of the conversation, then watched him hang up.

He handed me a slip of paper on which he'd written notes. "Dr. Hyram Ross' address is there at the bottom," he said. "Go see him today at two o'clock. And take Xanthea with you."

Thus began a series of sessions extending for weeks. Dr. Ross lit matches for Xanthea. He gave her matches

to light. Then he left matches within easy reach while
we watched through a two-way mirror from an adjoining room. But Xanthea's reaction seemed to be disinterest at best. In fact, she tended to withdraw from the
flames.

Dr. Ross was as baffled as Gordon and I had been.
Then for no apparent reason, Xanthea began telling us
a seemingly outlandish story. She described herself in
detail—a large woman, barely ambulatory. She described her surroundings, an old house in which her
room was on the second floor. She described her
clothes, fashions from the Victorian age. Then she described a night in which fire consumed the ancient
dwelling.

"I couldn't get out," she kept repeating.

Chills ran down my spine. I looked to Dr. Ross for an
answer. He merely shrugged.

Later that week, Xanthea and I were in the living
room. The boys were outside, playing on the lawn. But
Xanthea had decided to stay with me. I was in a chair
reading when I heard a crackling sound.

I looked up to see Xanthea leaning against the
French door, her tiny head pressed against the glass,
her eyes gazing off into space almost as if she were in a
trance. Suddenly, the carpet in an arc around her burst
into flame.

I nearly fainted.

I smothered the flames with a cushion, then with
hands fluttering like a leaf in a storm, I dialed Dr. Ross.
I was hysterical when he finally answered.

"Try to calm yourself," he soothed irritatingly. "Bring
Xanthea in right away. And try to stay calm."

I ran every red light and stop sign between our house
and his office. "I'm calm," I exclaimed as I burst into
his office.

Dr. Ross lifted Xanthea into his lap and played with
her for a long time. I sat nearby fidgeting. At last he got
down to business.

"Xanthea," he said, "do you remember the story you

told us the other day?"

Xanthea nodded.

What an intelligent little girl, I thought.

"The one about the lady burning up in the fire?"

"It was me," Xanthea said.

"Would you tell the story again?"

Xanthea nodded once more, then recited the tale nearly word-for-word as she had told it earlier.

"You understand that that happened a long time ago, don't you?" Dr. Ross asked.

Xanthea looked as if she wasn't entirely convinced.

"And that it can't happen again," he continued.

Xanthea stared at him without answering.

Dr. Ross carried Xanthea into another room. He avoided looking at me when he returned. He sat down at his desk and began scribbling in a file folder, then snapped it shut with finality.

"That's it?" I wondered aloud.

"I don't know," he answered, tearing a slip of paper from a tiny tablet. "This is something I don't understand. I've heard about it but I don't understand it."

He concentrated on the slip of paper upon which he was writing.

"I consulted with another psychiatrist, one who believes in this sort of thing . . . ."

"What sort of thing?"

"It's called paranormal phenomena, which means we don't know what the hell causes it. Specifically, this sort of phenomenon is referred to as reincarnation."

"Okay, I understand that. You think she remembers things that happened to her in a past life."

"I didn't say that. I don't know what I believe. All I'm saying is that according to my colleague, there have been reports of violent incidents like this one but that they don't seem to be common."

"That's reassuring."

"Usually, he says, when a child who has a manifestation of this nature tells someone about it, he forgets it and the incidents never recur."

"Incidents? You mean the fires."

Dr. Ross smiled patronizingly.

"Are you saying you think she created the fires with her mind?" I asked as calmly as I could under the circumstances.

He shrugged.

The room was silent a long time.

"No one knows for sure the power of the mind," he said. He trailed off as if embarrassed to be entertaining such outlandish notions.

"Is it over?" I was willing to settle for that even if I couldn't get an explanation.

"I don't know," he answered, looking at last into my face. "I hope so. All you can do is wait and see. In a week or so, casually ask if she remembers the story. If she doesn't, perhaps the worst is past. In the meantime, I want you to take this prescription and get it filled. It's for a sedative."

"For Xanthea?"

"No, for you."

I never got the prescription filled. But I never again had any difficulty sleeping. And we never again had any problems with mysterious fires.

Once in a while, though, it would give me a start when I'd see my daughter staring off into space, daydreaming. It reminded me of the day in the living room and it frightened me.

Soon it became obvious that true to form, she didn't even remember the story about the woman in the burning house. I asked her about it once. She just stared at me as if she thought I had been watching too much television.

My sigh of relief was a short one, however. Just when Xanthea seemed a once more normal two-year-old, her twin brother came forward with an equally shattering revelation.

We were on our way from Lake Bay to Gordon's office in Tacoma one afternoon—Gordon was taking us out to dinner. Jason was reading aloud from a picture book in the back seat. Nicholas and Xanthea were listening quietly in the seat beside me.

I had come to a stop at a railroad crossing as the guard rail slowly descended across my path. I, too, was getting caught up in Jason's story. But as the fast-moving train raced past in front of us, Nicholas let out a howl like a wounded wolf.

Suddenly, he was all elbows and knees as he frantically scrambled to climb over the seat toward his terrified brother.

"What's the matter?" I shouted, making a grab for Nicholas.

"Whatzamatter?" Jason echoed.

"Whatzamatter?" Xanthea added.

Now I was drawing Nicholas back across the seat. I cradled him, kicking and scratching, in my arms, alternating between asking "What is it?" and assuring him that "It's all right."

Red faced, his eyes bugged out in terror and rage, Nicholas gasped out his fears. "We were in Switzerland. We were skiing. And on the way back the tracks were icy and the train couldn't stop."

"What happened?" I asked urgently.

Nicholas faced me with a look of dumbfounded outrage. "I WAS KILLED!" he shouted.

By now the train was past. The cars behind me were honking.

"Okay, okay, okay," I said, surprised I was so articulate, under the circumstances.

Cars were passing on the shoulder to the right.

"It's okay, Nicky," I said. "The train is gone now."

Slowly, Nicholas stopped shaking. I noticed the cold stares of the drivers of other cars as they passed. I could feel Nicholas' muscles going lax and at last I let him go. He slumped in the seat beside me, only raising his eyes to glance nervously in both directions as we proceeded across the tracks.

It would take us months to help him overcome his fear of trains. As with a child who has nearly drowned, we introduced him to the water gradually. We bought him an electric train set. I took him to depots and stood hand in hand with him while the trains pulled in—a painful experience for both of us, since he invariably crushed my fingers into a single digit. At last, we took him for a short train ride.

He has never said for sure, but I still don't think he is particularly fond of trains, though I am convinced he no longer remembers why. He, too, forgot the story once he had told it.

Two down and one to go, I calculated. I began to watch Jason suspiciously out of the corner of my eye, looking, I assume, for telltale signs. But Jason and Gordon consistently proved to be what Gordon affectionately referred to as the "sane" ones in the family. A bat and a ball and someone to hit it to are all Jason has ever asked out of life.

Apparently, if he ever passed this way before, the experience left no lasting scars on his psyche.

Yet the series of events and my conscious fear that it would happen again left me nervous and on edge.

Perhaps that's the reason I fulfilled Gordon's prophesy. It began innocently enough.

I invited Dominic Dianco and his fiance to dinner one Saturday night. Dominic was our butcher.

I've always had a soft spot for steak, medium rare, but that wasn't why I took such a liking to Dominic. He was more than just our butcher. He was my friend. Normally, I didn't do the grocery shopping, but I bought our meat because I enjoyed chatting with Dominic. The first time I had gone into his shop, he had come from behind the counter to introduce himself. "You tell me what you want," he said, "and I'll be sure you get it."

He was warm, gregarious and as good as his word.

When I called at five o'clock on a Thursday and asked for filets enough to feed nine people at dinner that night, he would make a special trip to be sure I had them half an hour later. But he wasn't considerate of just friends and customers. He treated everyone like that.

Now, Dominic was having trouble and I wanted to let him know I cared.

Dominic had been married for more than thirty years. I had met his wife only once but once was enough. She spent the entire time finding fault with her husband. Not for sins I would find intolerable—philandering, sloth, drunkenness, brutality. His failure was an inability to amass great wealth. Perhaps the affluence around her had distorted her perspective, but I vowed I would never again allow myself to be closeted with such a shrew.

Dominic, too, had apparently had enough. He was going against the laws of his church by divorcing her. And if that alone wasn't sufficient grounds to raise eyebrows among some of Lake Bay's righteous citizens, he had already selected a new wife for himself.

Elizabeth Ethridge was a large, Aryan-looking woman. I had seen her around since she moved onto a farm on the edge of town but had never been formally introduced. About all I really knew was that she was a widow.

Dominic's divorce had been finalized but he was still suffering rebukes from many of the townspeople and was feeling a pinch in the pocketbook as some turned away from his tiny shop. Perhaps they were embittered by the fact that his divorce had unleashed his former wife on the town as a whole, since from all reports she now had a habit of dropping in unannounced in search of solace and commiseration.

"Why don't you bring Elizabeth around sometime, Dom?" I asked one day as I was placing an order for one of our Saturday night dinner parties. "I'd like to meet her."

"You mean to your house?" he asked.

"Sure," I said. "Why not come to dinner Saturday night. We're having a few friends in. I'm sure you'd like them."

"Well, we'll see," he answered hesitantly.

Later, he called. "We would love to come," he said. "I'll send over some extra beef with your order."

"Be sure and add it to my bill," I answered.

He chuckled.

"I mean it," I said. "When I invite someone to be my guest, I expect them to be my guest. If it's not on the bill, I'll sic the health board on you and we both know you'd never survive an inspection."

He laughed then.

He billed me for the meat but he showed up at the door that Saturday night with two large bottles of imported red wine.

Elizabeth Ethridge was shy and quiet, and Dominic hovered over her like a teenager on his first date. I was delighted that they fit comfortably into the group of dinner guests.

We chatted as we sipped cocktails in the living room, then adjourned to dinner. I sat Elizabeth beside me and Dominic on the other side of her.

Over dinner we exchanged small talk and she promised to bring me a favorite lasagne recipe. Dessert had just been served when I turned suddenly to Elizabeth and asked, "Does the name Tinker mean anything to you?"

She blanched.

"I'm sorry if I said anything wrong," I added hurriedly, realizing the name had upset her. "I just had this fleeting thought, like a voice saying, "Oh God, Tinker, I've bought the farm."

"That's what my husband called me," Elizabeth answered, her voice choked, barely audible.

Tinker? I mused. Elizabeth was a big-boned woman. Attractive, but nonetheless a big woman. I would never have guessed anyone would call her "Tinker."

Suddenly, I realized tears were trickling down her cheeks. The heavy silver spoon fell from her hand, shattering the delicate, Belgian crystal dessert glass. A sob shuddered through her as she pushed herself from the table.

Dominic rose quickly, enfolding her in his arms. I glanced around the now-silent dining room. All eyes were turned in our direction. Slowly, I came to my senses.

"Let's go into the den," I whispered to Dominic, as I, too, rose from the table. "Go ahead with your dessert," I called to the others as we hurried from the dining room.

I poured Elizabeth a snifter of brandy and apologized over and over as she sipped quietly from the glass.

"I'm so sorry if I said something wrong," I mumbled, nearly in tears myself by this time. I looked up to discover Gordon watching thoughtfully from the door.

"It's all right," Elizabeth said at last. "It's not your fault."

Gordon emitted a disgusted sigh and closed the door or his way back to our other guests.

"My first husband was a military pilot," Elizabeth began, as if she owed me an explanation. "When he retired, we moved to California, where he took a job monitoring the gas lines from the air. We were saving up to buy ourselves a farm."

I could hear Gordon's warning in the back of my mind but I simply couldn't help myself.

"I don't understand this," I interrupted, gazing at Elizabeth for some clue to the meaning behind the words now spewing from my mouth. "I'm in an airplane—it's a small plane. It's flying under telephone wires and the plane is going to crash and I'm thinking, 'My God, Tinker, I've bought the farm.'"

"One day, his plane crashed and he was killed," Elizabeth sobbed.

I now recalled Navy pilots I had known referring to fatal crashes as "buying the farm" and felt even more insensitive than before. But at the same time, I was fascinated by the irony. The cynical military reference to death had in this case taken root in real soil; they had indeed intended to buy the farm.

Elizabeth brought me abruptly back to reality. "The

farm meant so much to him," she concluded, her voice fluttering, "that I bought my little farm here with his insurance money."

It seemed the dinner party would drag on forever.

At last, Elizabeth was herself once more, though Dominic still seemed shaken. We joined the others for coffee in the living room. Dominic and Elizabeth left a short time later. I spent the rest of the evening assuring guests that nothing serious was wrong and carefully avoiding a rehash of what had transpired behind the closed doors of the den.

Our last guest finally said goodnight and disappeared into the darkness. Gordon and I were alone. It was time for the dreaded confrontation I knew must come.

Gordon's smile eroded into a severe glare as the door closed. The muscles at the base of his jaw stood out in small knots.

"You can't do this to people, Shirlee," he hissed.

"I know," I moaned softly. "I know."

"You've got to promise you'll never do it again."

Tears burned my eyes and traced a path down along the corners of my mouth. "I won't," I said. And I meant it.

CHAPTER 4

As Boeing went, so went Gordon.

It was 1970 when a billboard showed up against the Seattle skyline. With cynical poignancy, it commented on the state of the economy around Puget Sound; "Will the Last Person to Leave Seattle Shut Off the Lights."

Boeing was dying, or so it seemed.

America's enthusiasm for the far-off war was waning. And so were orders for arms. Boeing had miscalculated. It had failed to anticipate the shift, had failed to gear up for production of planes for peace.

Boeing employees were laid off in 1969. The housing market was glutted with $60,000 houses on sale for $45,000, then $30,000 and finally as low as $15,000. The highways were thick with moving vans. Everyone wanted out, it seemed.

Many lost everything and a few got wealthy in the process. At least one realtor who had been only marginally successful sank every dime he could lay his hands on into dirt cheap housing. Within six months, he would become a millionaire as Seattle stumbled groggily from its death bed.

Gordon was not so lucky. He was among the losers.

We lost everything.

Hand-in-hand we stood one last time on the patio, listening to the waves, smelling the sea air, weeping with despair. Gordon had exhausted every avenue in his effort to ward off financial collapse. Like Pavlov's

dog, I had begun to respond to bells—but rather than
making me hungry, the sound of a ringing telephone
made me physically ill. We hoped each call would bring
a miracle, some salvation. Invariably, it was a creditor,
begging, then demanding.

Quietly, Gordon climbed aboard a Boeing 707 bound
for Boston. Perhaps he could raise some capital there,
he thought.

I would not see Gordon again for nearly three years.

When Boston turned up dry, he continued on to
Europe on the trail of rumors that money or business
could be raised there. By now, every three-letter bur-
eaucracy in America—with the possible exception of
the FBI and the CIA—was after him.

They couldn't catch up with him, so they came after
me. I was an officer in the corporation, after all, and as
such was liable for the debts of the company.

For the first time in my life, it seemed, I was depend-
ent on others for survival. I looked for a job, figuring my
family could take care of my children during the day.
Then I learned that most of what I earned would go to
pay off corporate debts.

I found a small house and went into hibernation.
What was I to do, I wondered. The few friends I allowed
close enough to share my misery suggested welfare.

"I'll die first," I answered, then marked them off my
list of acceptable companions.

After eating nothing but pancakes made with water
for three days in a row, I took the children with me to
the garage. There was parked our car—or what passed
for a car. It had been used by the company for running
errands; a third-hand vehicle that was little more than
a frame, an engine and a body as tattered as my spirit.
Not even our creditors had wanted it.

It seemed sufficient for my purposes.

I sat the children in the car and rolled down the
windows. Then I closed the garage door and turned on
the engine.

"Sit quietly," I told the children. "Be very still."

And so we sat.

Tears—perhaps of sadness, perhaps from the sting of the fumes—rolled down my cheeks.

"In a moment, we will go," I told the children.

I felt myself begin to drift. All the faces I had ever known and some I had not yet met flickered before my mind's eye, their mouths moving but no sound coming from them.

Suddenly, a voice broke through, a voice I didn't recognize, not even as my own.

"You have no right!" it shouted.

My eyes jerked open. Slowly—oh, so slowly—I gazed around me. The children were nodding sleepily.

There was no one elese in the car, no one else in the garage. Just me and my conscience. I tried to ignore the voice. I told myself death was the best thing for all of us. But the insistent voice shattered my concentration. I surrendered to it. I had no right, I admitted.

As if through a strong current, my hand moved to the key and turned it off, I called to the children to awaken them and climbed heavily from the car. The garage door seemed to weigh a ton but at last it too gave way before my suddenly revived will to live.

I should have taken the children to the hospital to be sure I had done them no harm. I was too ashamed, too terrified. I watched over them all night, drinking coffee to stay awake. I prayed and listened to their breathing. Periodically, I vomited.

Next morning, I did what I thought I never would have courage to do. I went to the welfare office.

I had been a snob.

I guess I still was.

How can these people dress so shabbily, I wondered. Where is their pride?

Then I realized I was there for exactly the same reason they were. It is hard to overcome stereotypes.

Giving had always come easily for me, especially in recent years when I had so much to give. Receiving was more difficult, especially charity.

Yet now I found myself looking at welfare from both sides. On one hand, I couldn't divorce myself from the feeling that if these people wanted work, they could find it. But on the other hand, I was one of them, no better, no worse.

Many American taxpayers bemoan the money they pay to support welfare, but few will ever know the cost to those who receive the paltry checks, the ones who really need it and would give anything not to. With every check you receive, your heart gets a little poorer.

I was determined I would get off welfare as soon as I could. But first I had to get on it.

One of the counselors brought me into his office. He was a kindly, balding, red-faced little man who could see I was dying of humiliation. With a benevolent smile, he issued me $150 worth of food stamps, then handed me a fistful of tickets to the Ringling Brothers Circus which would be in Seattle the following week.

As I gazed at those tickets, I realized it had not been me taking care of the children all those weeks, but they who were caring for me. It seemed so long since they had experienced moments of joy, since any of us had.

For a week we talked of nothing but the circus. And when it arrived, it was even grander than I recalled from my childhood. For two hours we feasted our imaginations on tumblers and pachaderms and gaudy clowns.

Then it was over and we were back once more in our tiny home.

I sat motionless for days before our television screen. It was my companion from sign-on to sign-off. We had no telephone. We couldn't afford one. We didn't need one. I had shunned all my friends; I didn't want to talk to anyone.

But a few people like Joy Sponaguel refused to be put off by my anger and my pride. She would stop by and turn off the TV, then order me from the apartment.

"You're getting prison pallor," she would shout. "Your skin's beginning to look like the belly of a fish."

She would drag me out into the sunlight and force me to admit I was still alive.

There was some unseen force linking us, something I later learned to call telepathy. Sitting before the television, I would suddenly feel a compulsion to speak to Joy. So I'd walk the two blocks to the nearest pay phone and dial her number.

The phone never rang more than once. Joy would be waiting for me.

"How'd you know I was going to call?" I asked her one day.

"Because I wanted you to," she answered.

The fact that her response put the question to rest is a reflection of my confused state at the time. When she wanted me to call, I automatically called—it seemed perfectly natural. Why challenge it?

Even Mother accepted it as simple fact. She found our communication system far more efficient than AT&T's. Besides that it gave her a way of keeping in touch with me when I didn't want to be in touch. Whenever she wanted to talk to me, she'd call Joy and tell her to have me call home.

One day when Joy stopped by to air me out, we walked around the block a couple of times, then settled down in my kitchen for a cup of ersatz coffee. I was pouring us a second cup when Joy pulled a packet from her purse and laid it in front of me.

"Maybe it's time to do what you are supposed to do," she said.

"What do you mean?" I asked as I eyed what was obviously a deck of cards. I opened the box and spread the odd looking cards across the table.

"They're tarot cards," Joy said. "Take a bus to the library and get a book on tarot. It's what you're meant to do."

After Joy left, I put the cards on my bureau and headed back to the TV. I might be sitting yet if the appliance store hadn't repossessed the television a week later.

Without a TV or radio in the house, I began reading everything I could find; anything to escape the crushing weight of my reality. I read every book I owned, then everything I could borrow from friends and neighbors. At last I turned to the Renton Public Library, where I read everything that struck me as remotely interesting. There I discovered a small collection of books on tarot.

Tentatively, I read them. Hungrily, I reread them.

Despite the eerie events of my past, I had persisted in my belief that what Xanthea's psychiatrist called the paranormal was nothing more than mind over matter with an able assist from imagination and fresh accidents.

Tarot readers, I believed, were akin to river boat gamblers, experts at the fast shuffle.

But here I was reading books by serious authors who were convinced that in the right hands the tarot unlocked the power to forecast and to enlighten. It was the hands that were important, I discovered.

I had always been amused when friends told me they had found a tarot reader. Why not just buy a deck and read your own cards, I wondered. Now I knew. Not everyone has the gift. And those who do possess it usually find it impossible to objectively read for themselves.

The cards are a focusing tool, a means of triggering extrasensory perception. Each card and every combination of cards have meanings which arouse insights in the gifted reader, creating a whole far greater than the sum of its parts.

I wanted to be a gifted reader. I played with my cards, shuffling and reshuffling the deck, learning to lay the pasteboard pictures in spreads, studying their meanings, sorting out the images that formed in my mind. It was a slow process.

At first friends stopped by unannounced for readings, more out of curiosity than confidence in me. But slowly, I developed a reputation for accuracy; why else would anyone come back a second time to sit through an hour and a half reading that should have taken only an hour?

My friends were patient with me and I was reaping the benefits of their patience. I was coming out of my shell.

I looked back, wondering how long I had been in seclusion. It had been nearly a year since I had seen Gordon. I missed him and I needed him. I had written him weekly and had gotten periodic terse, frustrated letters in return.

I thought about Xan.

Had he abandoned me, too?

Perhaps I hadn't kept the faith. He had warned us in those last months. "The end is near," he had said. "Prepare for it. Or avoid it."

It may seem hard to believe in financial counseling from the spirit world, yet that's exactly what Xan was offering. He foretold the impending financial collapse and offered us salvation. In less worldly terms, he told us to cut our overhead and to expand our client list, taking a loss on smaller accounts to insure a broad base representing steady income when disaster struck at Boeing.

But by then Gordon and I had tasted success. We had confidence in ourselves. We did it our way.

Xan must be having a belly laugh in some celestial counting house, I mused.

I began to look to the future, puzzling over how I could pull myself and my family together, how I could settle old accounts and become gainfully employed, how I could get off welfare.

One day as I sat at the kitchen table attempting a reading on myself, trying to discover if my cards would tell me how to proceed, I found myself invariably turning up the death card. Of itself, the death card is not evil. But in conjunction with certain others, it can be ominous.

No matter how many times I shuffled, those ominous

combinations came up. A shiver ran through me and suddenly I felt compelled—more compelled than I could remember—to call Joy.

I literally ran to the pay phone and with shaking fingers dropped in my dime.

"What is it?" I shouted when Joy answered.

"It's your father," she said sadly. "He has been killed." His car had been hit by a train. Perhaps the best that could be said about his death was it had been quick.

Now, Mother was all alone, living in Gordon's and my honeymoon bungalow. When Gordon and I moved out, we sold it to my sister who had been renting it to my folks.

"Come live with me," Mother said. "We'll pool our resources. We'll get along."

My life had gone full circle. Once more I was back in Eunice's house, the house I had left with such fanfare four years earlier. I recalled a message from Xan, one that came to me during one of my poor-little-rich-girl bouts of depression.

"They bring you to your knees," he had said.

I had been brought to my knees. But I would learn to stand again.

I have read many times that the ancients believed celibacy was important in the development of psychic ability, that sexual energy can be transformed into psychic energy, that one area of the psyche must lie dormant if another is to mature rapidly. During this phase of my life, I had a lot of energy to devote to psychic pursuits.

Gordon's letters came with increasing regularity now. They were warm and affectionate but lacking the confidence that had been one of his most appealing characteristics. Nonetheless, the letters we shared held us together.

I missed Gordon, his touch, his taste, his smell, the assurance of his caress. A woman needs a man, especially in the dark stillness when a bed can be the loneliest place on earth. She needs a place to warm her feet, but more important, a place to warm her heart.

I never dated during Gordon's absence, though like every reluctant dieter, I looked at the menu. I exercised my willpower. I abstained.

I endured the nights alone.

I endured the days with Mother's help, stretching them to their limit before tumbling under the weight of mindless exhaustion into sleep.

We survived, the five of us—Mother, Jason, Xanthea, Nicholas and I. Mother had a little money from Father's insurance, pension and social security. I continued receiving welfare and hoping I would soon be out from under corporate debts.

An attorney who was an old family friend offered to see what he could do. And so began a blizzard of legal correspondence that would go on for years.

I occupied myself with my cards.

Friends told other friends I could read and those friends brought complete strangers. I didn't mind. I've always enjoyed meeting people. And the people they brought were fascinating.

There were housewives looking for a better life or proof that their husbands were philandering. There were bookies and bankers and brain surgeons and stock brokers.

They came in pin-striped suits and conservative tweeds, sparkling with expensive jewelry and success. They smoked cigars and pipes and imported cigarettes, and sipped thoughtfully at wine I could ill afford but bought anyway as the price I paid for their company.

I was flattered but at the same time perplexed that everyone from criminals to congressmen seemed willing to alter his life on the basis of what a deck of cards read by a woman in Federal Way, Washington, had to say.

The responsibility seemed awesome. But once the cards were dealt, my terror would evaporate. I became nothing more than a conduit for the messages I saw there.

Periodically, though, I would censor those messages. I refused to be the harbinger of more grief than I believed the person for whom I was reading could handle. I agree with those who say such predictions can become self-fulfilling prophecies.

By now I was doing as many as half a dozen readings a week. I could have been doing more—our phone was ringing nearly constantly as more asked to be put on the waiting list—but the process still came hard for me. It was mentally and emotionally fatiguing.

So was the fact that I still hadn't figured out a way to make money.

Then one night, a mathematics professor from the University of Washington laid a $5 bill in front of me as I concluded his reading.

"What's that for?" I laughed.

"For the reading," he answered with puzzlement.

I was amused, then offended.

I felt like a prostitute.

"I can't take that," I said emphatically. For a fleeting instant that crisp bill seemed a talisman capable of magically robbing me of the power I had been working so hard to develop.

He seemed embarrassed now.

"I've always paid," he stammered. "I meant no disrespect."

"You've never paid here," I said sharply, stuffing the bill into his jacket pocket.

I worried over the proposition for days, terrified I would surrender to the temptation to take money for what I was doing. It was bad enough I had to do readings in my bedroom—neighbors curious about all the men they saw coming and going at odd hours had been told by my children that they weren't sure what I did, but that I did it in my bedroom with the door closed.

Did other psychics charge, I wondered. The professor had assured me they took money for their services, but I found that hard to believe.

At last I telephoned the only psychic I knew of, a wizened old man known only as Doc Anderson, the subject of an article I had recently read. I was surprised that with no more to go on than that, I got his number quickly from the information operator in the town in Tennessee where he lived.

He listened patiently as I recounted my fears. Then he chuckled as my grandfather had chuckled the day I told him about the little men I thought were living in my closet.

"Of course, my dear girl," he said with a reassuring wheeze, "accept the money. If you take care of the gift, the gift will take care of you."

That was good enough for me.

I turned pro.

I started charging clients $5.00 per reading, which amounted to about $5.00 per hour as long as I was working. I was getting faster, but I still read one card at a time. It took me a full 60 minutes to get through a single spread.

I didn't charge really close friends—it seemed that one reading was all it took to form lasting relationships. That fact, coupled with the lingering fatigue reading caused, slowed down the profits. Yet I was convinced I could make a living and decide to declare my independence. I went off welfare.

It was a bittersweet parting of the ways; I recalled that for many months, standing in line at the welfare office had been the high point in my social life.

Now I had something else to fill my life. And my pocketbook.

The first year, I raked in a total of $1,005. Not much by anyone's standards, but enough to keep my pride and family intact. Over the next five years, my salary would double annually.

I scrimped and saved until I had enough to bring Gordon home. My attorney friend said Gordon wasn't out of the woods yet, but that things had died down sufficiently that perhaps together we could work our way free.

We would work our way free.

But it would be our last major accomplishment together.

Gordon came home to face the music. But it wasn't the home he had left behind. Nor was I the same woman or he the same man. The world had turned over many times in the nearly three years we were apart.

We still loved one another but we were no longer in love. He would remain a dear and important part of my life. A loving friend, but not a lover. And not a husband.

CHAPTER 6

There are objects I have touched in my lifetime—objects that have touched me—which I would just as soon leave to those who can handle the terror. I can't.

The first time I learned how frightened I can be was several months before Gordon returned from Europe. Fay Suttles had learned Gordon was coming home at last and decided we should celebrate.

"We're going out on the town," she said over the phone one afternoon. "Get yourself gussied up; my treat."

I attempted to beg off.

It had been so long since I had been out that I wasn't sure I would know how to act. What I was sure of, though, was that I didn't have anything to wear.

I had sold the best of my wardrobe when the empire collapsed. The finest gown in my closet was a long, burgundy dress Mother had made for me. I had never worn it, though. It was a bit too grand for scuffling around the house in. Yet I wasn't convinced it was right for the nightspots of Seattle.

"I haven't a thing to wear," I swore. But Fay knew better. She and Mother were old friends, too old it seems sometimes.

"Wear the dress your mother made you."

"But I don't have anything to wear with it."

"I'll bring the accessories."

I had run out of counter-arguments.

So there I sat in my burgundy gown at 7 p.m., my

nails drying to a shimmering red, my cheeks blushed, my eyes shadowed and my lips properly rouged. All I needed now were a pair of shoes, a handbag and some jewelry.

I felt uncomfortable waiting there, a feeling I sometimes get just before receiving bad news. Probably jitters over going out, I reasoned and tried to squeeze them from my mind. But the longer I waited, the more anxious I got.

When Fay and her husband Ole Olson arrived, I took a long deliberate draw on my cigarette and slipped on the shoes Fay had brought with her. Fay pinned my bodice with an antique looking broach and I tried on several of her rings before deciding on the ones I would wear.

Then I noticed the evening bag Fay had laid on the coffee table in front of me. It was perfect, exactly the shade of my gown.

I picked it up as I started to rise, then quickly dropped it on the floor and fell back into the stuffed chair.

"My God, Fay," I shrieked, "that's not your purse!"

It was as if a movie had just been projected on the back of my brain. it was not a pleasant film.

It involved murder and had been shot from the perspective of the victim. I could feel myself walking along a high bank at the edge of an industrial area. With me was a sailor, at least I though he was a sailor. He wore a pea jacket and watch cap, anyway.

I could hear no voices, but knew we were arguing. Suddenly, he grabbed my arm and jerked me around. His eyes were aflame with rage. His hands groped for my throat as I tried to pull away. I fought, oh, how I fought. I pummeled his face and chest, scratched at his eyes, gripped his wrists, in an effort to break his hold.

I could feel my lungs exploding within my chest.

And then I died.

Fay and Ole stood watching uncertainly as I drew myself into a shivering ball away from the burgundy purse that lay there on the floor like a science fiction flower capable at any moment of transforming into some odious monster.

I told them about the sensation I had received from the purse and tears began trickling down Fay's cheeks. Ole scooped up the purse and walked from the house.

"You're right, Shirlee," Fay said. "It's not my purse."

It had belonged to her sister, she explained. Her sister had been slain by a sailor in Tacoma in 1949, she added softly.

I tried to recall if I'd ever heard the story but couldn't. Mother, who had been attracted by my shriek, was standing in the livingroom doorway. I asked if she'd known about the slaying.

She shook her head.

For a long time I puzzled over the story, wondering if I'd heard it then, forgotten until something about the purse brought it all back. Eventually, I would come to accept the fact that what I had seen had come entirely from the purse, the purse Fay's sister had been carrying the night she died.

The phenomenon is called psychometry—the ability to divine facts about an object or its owner through contact with it. Sometimes contact isn't even necessary; just being near it is enough.

Over the next several years, I would learn to avoid anything even remotely connected with violence. The sensation scared the hell out of me.

I admire psychics such as New Jersey housewife Dorothy Allison and a St. Louis housewife named Bevy Jaeger who have the guts to psychometrize in an effort to help police solve grisly crimes.

Mrs. Allison, who has worked with police throughout the nation, is perhaps the best known psychic sleuth. Her success rate is incredible.

Less widely heralded but equally successful is Bevy, the first professional psychic to hold a private investigator's license.

Police work came naturally to her. Her father, grandfather and uncles were in law enforcement.

But psychic ability didn't come so easily.

"I was the stupidest person in the world as far a ESP went," she says. "I didn't know how to do anything. I'd never had a psychic dream, a psychic hunch or a successful bet at the horseraces."

Then, in the mid-1960s, she became fascinated by reports on research behind the Iron Curtain. She read everything she could find on the subject. But mere reading wasn't enough—she wanted to do the things she read about.

For days, weeks, months, she sat quietly practicing such things as "feeling" the colors on painted cards, or "testing" the difference between salt and sugar by holding the substances in her hand.

She developed her abilities gradually. Initially, she learned to predict newspaper headlines a day in advance and to guess what was in the mail before it was delivered. And she began to sort daydreams from meaningless impressions. Then she learned to interpret those impressions.

By fall 1971, she was not only convinced of her own ability but was sure she could teach others. That's what she was doing when she was consulted in the mysterious disappearance of a St. Louis woman named Sally Lucas.

Holding a nightgown and powder puff that had belonged to the missing woman, Bevy came up with impressions that later proved strikingly accurate.

She saw a short woman with medium length hair and felt pain in the right side of her head and neck. Mrs. Lucas was short, with medium length hair. Later it would be determined that she died from a blow to the right side of her head.

Bevy had a vision of a car abandoned near water and saw it being examined by a patrolman. Next day, police recovered Mrs. Lucas' car near a beach in Florida.

The letter "C," an airplane and the head of a horse flashed through her mind. Mrs. Lucas's body was later discovered close to Spirit of St. Louis Airport in St.

Louis, near Highway C and CC, at the edge of Wild Horse Creek Road.

"It was amazing the number of things she said that turned out to be true," a Missouri Highway Patrol captain told a St. Louis reporter.

A short time after her work in the Lucas case, Bevy organized the PSI Squad—a network of psychics, primarily former students, to consult with police throughout the country.

"I got the private investigator's license because I was told it would make it easier to testify in court," she muses. "But so far, I've never been called to testify."

Psychics have testified in England, but thus far their testimony remains inadmissible in American courts.

I agree with the American practice. I do not believe it is necessary for psychics to testify; I am convinced they should never be allowed to stand up in a court of law, point across the courtroom and shout, "That's him!"

It is impossible for even the best and most conscientious among us to guarantee against prejudices in our interpretation of images we receive. Each of us carries in his subconscious a criminal stereotype which could easily affect judgment in cases of criminal identification. That's why I feel the best use of psychics is in helping come up with evidence—solid evidence—which can be verified by police and which in turn can lead police to suspects.

Evidence, rather than positive identification, is usually what's available through psychics anyway. No psychics with whom I am aquainted receive the type of visions portrayed in films and on television. They do not stand back, watching a crime reenacted before the mind's eye, then clutch their hearts and gasp, "I know who killed Aunt Martha!"

My first experience was unusual in that I saw the event unfold sequentially. Yet I could not see the face of my killer. It is as if in the moment of death, the victim blotted all traces from her consciousness.

More typical of the information gained through psy-

chometry is the series of jumbled images Bevy recorded
in the Sally Lucas investigation. In fact, many psychic
insights come in the form of scattered abstractions
which are difficult to interpret, especially when you
have no direct contact with the events or individuals
involved.

Early in the 1968 presidential campaign, I told
friends at a cocktail party I believed whoever was
elected would not survive his presidency. While reading
news reports about the campaigns, I had recurring sensations of doom, the image of a smoking revolver, the
ominous feeling associated with scandal and suicide.
The word coverup ran through my mind again and
again. I was convinced that whoever was elected would
kill himself in the oval office as a result of a scandal I
could not envision.

It was only after Watergate, after Nixon had resigned
in disgrace, that one of those who had been present at
the party reminded me how wrong I had been.

Criminal investigations are even more difficult. It is
often impossible to tell how and even if images relate to
the crime in question.

I believe I could develop my psychometry to the point
that I could learn to pick up many more details. But I
don't want to. In those visions, I am forever the victim,
and it is a feeling I do not enjoy.

Yet I have participated in murder investigations. The
first came in the wake of a series of gruesome slayings
for which Ted Bundy would eventually be accused.

Ted had seemed an innocuous fellow—a friend of my
friend Ann Rule, whose chronicle of his murder spree
stretching the breadth of the country would become a
bestseller. Ted and Ann had become aquainted while
working together on a telephone hotline counseling
service while he was a student at the University of
Washington and she was making a living as an author
of true detective stories. Ann proved more instrumental
in solving the case than I did. In fact, all I would be able
to contribute was the title of her book, *The Stranger*

Beside Me.

But that was still in the future.

In spring 1974, the Puget Sound area was in the grip of terror as young women were being brutally assaulted sexually, then slain; some of the victims had disappeared entirely.

The remains of several were discovered in woodland near Issaquah, 30 miles east of Seattle. Police were combing the terrain in search of clues and more pieces of the missing women.

I was asked by the team of law enforcement agencies heading up the investigation to visit the search site. I would be one of two psychics lending assistance, I was told.

Two young policemen picked me up at my home in Federal Way. They made no attempt to hide the fact that they were uncomfortable with the unorthodox approach their superiors had chosen.

"We're not sure what to expect," one of them said as he studied me head to toe. Obviously, he hadn't expected to find me dressed in a business suit, complete with gloves.

If he had been looking for someone a bit more exotic—in the mold of the hocus-pocus approach to psychic phenomena—I had disappointed him. But he wouldn't be disappointed long.

As we drove to the outskirts of Renton to pick up our second psychic, I explained that I was a novice at crime busting. The men in blue seemed pleased that I was willing to admit I was no more sure whether I would be of help than they were.

I asked what the investigation had turned up so far but they said they had orders not to say. They even apologized for leaving me in the dark.

I would soon learn that police are hesitant about sharing information for fear it will contaminate the impressions of psychics involved in investigations.

The reasoning is sound. Unfortunately, that secretiveness generally extends far beyond an investigation, meaning it can be months, sometimes years after a case has been tried before the psychic learns if he was at all helpful.

We chatted as the squad car rattled along a gravel road, then up a dirt path before coming to a halt behind a beat up pickup truck with a bumper sticker proclaiming: "Goat Lovers of the World Unite."

We walked uncertainly up the cracked walkway toward the ramshackle house. One of the policemen knocked at the door.

It was opened by a man with no teeth and a protruding nose that nearly touched his chin. "Lizzie be ready in a minute," he announced as he motioned us inside. He shooed a goat off the couch and his wife offered coffee which we politely declined.

Our second psychic, it turned out, was the sister of our toothless host. She had come to town from the high country expressly to help find the sex slayer.

While we waited for her to appear, the lady of the house showed off her collection of empty Avon bottles. Then, just when I thought nothing could make me any more uncomfortable, Madame Lizzie swept into the room, the train of her black gown trailing in giant billows behind her. Her feet were noticeably bare and noticeably dirty. But her face was well covered—with a month's supply of cosmetics. Atop her head was a giant turban.

All she needed was a crystal ball, I mused, glancing around the room to see if one was present. Crystal balls and tarot cards have an important role in psychic phenomena, not because they have any magical qualities, but because they serve as focusing tools, points of concentration for the gifted psychic. Such stereotypical paraphernalia as flowing gowns do not, however. They cheapen the gift, reducing it to nothing more than carnival antics. I have always abhorred the pretense so often associated with my chosen profession but never more than at that moment.

We quickly dispensed with introductions, then the

policemen and I scrambled for the car, Madame Lizzie close on our heels. I was dying as the policeman at the wheel maneuvered through traffic on our way to the Issaquah burial ground. I could see him in the rearview mirror rolling his eyes heavenward to punctuate mumbled remarks to his companion.

I'm not going to survive this, I was thinking when Madame Lizzie's voice exploded right next to my ear. "Stop!" she screeched.

The policeman in the passenger seat jerked his head around, his face rigid with anticipation. I'm not sure but I believe his hand dropped instinctively to the butt of his revolver. His partner, meanwhile, was attempting to shove the brake pedal through the floor and I was sinking lower in my seat.

Madame Lizzie merely rubbed her forehead—the third eye as it's known in the trade. Her mortal eyes were clinched tight. "I'm picking up vibrations," she whispered before launcing into a stacatto of the top 20 psychic cliches.

"You feeling anything, Shirlee?" asked the policeman in the passenger's seat.

"Just humiliation," I thought and shook my head.

For more than an hour we drove in stops and starts around Issaquah as Madame Lizzie worked at homing in on the signals only she was receiving. To every question from the officers in the front seat, she answered, "Shhhh!" Psychic detective work takes a lot of concentration, I decided.

I did what I could to help. I honestly tried to tune in on the sensations she professed to be receiving. I had telephoned other psychics around the country, colleagues I had met through correspondence. Most had described the sensation I should be looking for as a chill, an eerie coolness in the air.

Madame Lizzie was still Sarah Bernhardting and I was feeling as if this entire fruit fly expedition had been a monumental waste of time when I felt the change. I can't describe the feeling as coolness, exactly, though I

did feel a chill. It was more like a sudden change in
barometric pressure, the swift variation that preceeds a
summer storm.

"Stop here, please," I said softly. We were at a cross-
road on the outskirts of town. On one corner stood the
remains of an ancient motor lodge, much like the one
Claudette Colbert and Clark Gable visited in *It Happened One Night*. Otherwise, there was nothing but
farmland as far as the eye could see.

What was left of three lodges stood in a row amid the
high grass. It has been a long time since anyone had
spent money to stay here. Yet I was certain something
evil had happened in this location.

It hadn't happened in these buildings, however. I
wandered past them, drawn along an overgrown path
across a culvert.

"Here," I said, and for a fleeting moment felt as if I
were caught in a time warp. Nothing looked the same.
It was late night and before me loomed a large building,
a roadhouse surrounded by late 1930s and 1940s model
cars. An orange neon sign blinked in the window. My
heart pounded to the rhythm of swing music drifting to
me from inside.

I was terrified. Something, someone was there in the
darkness waiting for me. I backed between a black
Studebaker and a tan Ford like one my father owned
when I was a girl. I could feel myself drifting between
the conflicting images of my own memories and this
unfamiliar scene.

I wanted to scream but knew any sound would leave
me vulnerable to whatever it was that stalked me. I
stumbled against the side of the Studebaker and in that
instant felt a living thing brush against me.

Then I saw its fist, large and dark and hard. In the
fist was a knife rising above my head, only to come
hurtling down into my flesh, again and again.

I was nearly hysterical when the two young policemen dragged me back to reality, helping me to the car
where Madame Lizzie sat with her eyes glazed shout-

ing, "Yes, yes, I feel it now. . . ."

I felt like a fool as they drove me home.

The closest I had come to helping solve a modern crime was reliving a crime that had happened at least a quarter of a century earlier—if it happened at all. I took a sedative and tumbled fully clothes onto my bed.

It was late in the evening when my mother awoke me to say one of the nice young policemen had called to say the crossroads where we had stopped had once been the site of a roadside tavern. It also had been the scene of several unsolved slayings, he had added. I had once more demonstrated that while I may not be good at solving crimes, I make an excellent victim.

But I had also demonstrated one of the most unnerving problems facing psychics attempting to help solve violent crimes. The vibrations—perhaps electricity would more appropriately describe the energy—created by acts of violence lingers at the scene for ages. This fact adds to the complexity of separating events, of knowing which images go with which crimes.

There would be other investigations in which I would be asked to help the police. I don't wish to recall them here or anywhere ever again.

Many remain unsolved—though police and I believe we know who committed them, there just isn't sufficient evidence to convict those responsible. Others were successfully prosecuted but those who were convicted are still among the living.

To discuss these crimes in detail would be a public admission of my involvement in their investigation and that is something I cannot do. I am as frightened by the potential consequences as I am by the prospect of reliving the experience.

My work with police has, however, taught me a great deal about my own psychic talents. I am not as good as either Dorothy Allison or Bevy Jaeger at psychic sleuthing and hope never to be. But I have demonstrated an ability I believe can sometimes make me just as valuable.

I have a faculty for interpreting information accumulated by other psychics, for weeding out the irrelevant from the consequential.

Given the notes or transcripts of tapes produced by these psychics, I can tell police which clues are important to the case under investigation.

This may be related to another skill I discovered I possess. It enables me to find fabrications in written testimony. I guess it would be more accurate to say the skill was discovered by an attorney who was among my clients.

He asked me one day if I would mind looking at depositions taken in a frustrating manslaughter case he was defending. The case involved his client, who was accused of negligence in a three-car wreck in which two people died.

The depositions were rife with contradictions and he hoped I might be able to figure out who—if anyone—was lying.

I was fascinated by the challenge.

I sat for hours scanning line after numbered line, page after page. At first, I could tell my friend nothing. Then after three days, sentences began to jump out at me as if they were printed in slightly heavier type. I marked the sentences with a red pen, then moved on.

Armed with these depositions, the attorney began looking for evidence which would disprove the red-marked statements. In some cases, he found what he was looking for. In others, he relied on examinations of the witnesses to bring out the truth.

Later, he would tell me that he was able to demonstrate that 80 percent of the sentences I identified as questionable were either outright lies or a matter of perception.

Over the course of two years, I supplemented my income by reading depositions. Word spread among the legal fraternity and I was soon turning business away.

Eventually, though, I quit. It was driving me crazy. I cannot think of a more boring or more tedious way to make a living.

Yet I believe there are people who are emotionally and intellectually equipped to enjoy that sort of job. And I also believe that when psychic phenomena are sufficiently understood and accepted, there will be ways of training individuals to perform this service.

By the same token, I believe that this liberation of the psychic force will lead to psychic training in such professions as law enforcement and medicine.

Many of the police with whom I have come in contact are natural psychics, though they dismiss their insights as hunches. Not all their talent comes from experience, however. Nor does a doctor's I know. He can tell the moment I walk into his office what is ailing me. He then confirms his diagnosis with tests. Privately, he admits he has no other explanation for the diagnosis than that he instinctively knows what is afflicting me and most other patients. He claims the talent is not unique—many other doctors have it as well, he says.

Publicly, however, he is pragmatic. He admits nothing. Who in his right mind is going to jeopardize his professional standing by saying he believes his insights are grounded in the supernatural?

Some day, perhaps. But not yet.

CHAPTER 7

Gordon had come and gone. It had been immediately apparent to both of us that what we had once had, we had no more. We remain the best of friends and he will always be the father of my children. But he could never again fill the void in me, nor I the one in him.

He would eventually win his battle with the bill collectors and the taxmen. We would pay off his debts and he would begin anew with a business in Portland, Oregon.

I would continue reading tarot cards.

I was still fascinated by those who came to me, the tales they had to tell, the reasons for their quests. Sometimes, though, it could be unnerving.

A client had given me a gift, a dog we called Frankie. It was alleged that Frankie was a full-blooded poodle, but I was always convinced there was a terrier hidden somewhere in his background. I thanked my benefactor as profusely as I could under the circumstances.

The children loved the scraggly little beast but I had difficulty warming to him. In fact, I tried on several occasions to give him away. Once, I offered him to a close friend.

"I don't need a dog, Shirlee," she protested.

"Take him," I demanded as I shoved the puppy into her arms, "or I'll put a curse on you."

My friend studied the mangey animal for a long time, then answered, "I'll take the curse."

Eventually, I would grow attached to Frankie. But there was one quality I never quite accepted—his compulsion to bark whenever anyone came into the house. He would begin yapping as soon as the doorknob turned, run through the house spreading the alarm, then race back to the door to bark and feint at the intruder.

Usually the intruder was a member of the family, but that didn't deter Frankie—familiarity bred contempt.

The only time I know of that Frankie did not break into a howl when the front door opened occurred one summer day. I was alone in the house at the time, just climbing out of the shower, when I glanced at the bathroom door. There stood the largest woman I had ever seen in my life. And beside her stood Frankie, tail wagging.

"Hello," I said, my voice rich with discomfort. "How are you?"

"The gypsies say I killed my mother," the woman answered. "The police think I did it too. But I didn't— she fell down the stairs on her own."

Had Frankie been telepathic, he would have known that he was going to get his, and I was going to give it to him.

I smiled.

"Why don't you have a seat in the living room," I suggested. "I'll be right out as soon as I get dressed."

"I'll wait," she said. She didn't budge.

"Well," I apologized, "it's a little strange standing here naked before someone I don't even know."

"Don't worry about it. You haven't got anything I haven't seen before."

"No, I'm sure of that . . . ."

She allowed me to close the door part way and I toweled myself dry. I was putting on my bra when she stuck her head through the doorway.

"You always put your bra on that way?"

"Yes, I guess so."

She made a disgusted face and shook her head.

I put on the rest of my clothes as quickly as I could and stood gazing at myself in the mirror wondering what I was going to do next. The phone rang.

I bolted past the intruder and grabbed the receiver.

"Is this Shirlee Teabo?" asked the unfamiliar voice on the other end of the line.

"Oh, hello, dear," I answered.

"What?"

"Where are you now?"

"I'm in Puyallup."

"Well, on your way home. Why don't you pick up some fried chicken for lunch."

The caller hung up.

"I'll see you in a few minutes, then," I said and hung up too.

"Who was that?" the intruder demanded.

"My husband," I said. "He's on his way home now. He'll be here in just a little bit. Three minutes tops."

With that the woman grabbed the collar of my blouse.

"You stole my car keys!" she screamed. "What have you done with my keys?" There was insanity in the eyes inches from my face.

"I think you must be mistaken," I said between rattling teeth. "I think you left them in your car. But I'll take a look around in here just to be sure. You go look outside."

She went for it.

As soon as she was outside, I locked the door. Then I ran frantically through the house locking every other door and window that wasn't already bolted. I grabbed the phone and slid under the bed. I called the police and hid there while she pounded on the door.

Eventually, she went away.

Five minutes later, the police arrived and I spent a half hour reassuring them I wasn't a crackpot.

Not everyone who came to see me came with problems.

There was a group of six women all in their mid-70s who drove from a Des Moines retirement home on a regular basis. Only one was still spry enough to drive, but as long as she was mobile, all of them were.

I read the driver first. Mother served the others tea while they waited.

Mrs. Abercrombie, a Scorpio, was lovely in her blue bouffant hairdo. She had a mischievous grin that lit up the room when I spread the cards, then spread them again. For some reason, no matter how I dealt them, they indicated Mrs. Abercrombie was a disarmingly active old woman.

"I'm sorry," I said, "but the cards are in a playful mood."

"What do they say?" she asked in a gleeful whisper.

"Well," I stammered, "they indicate you've got a rather active sex life." I smiled wanly and reshuffled the cards.

"Hell, Honey," she beamed, " the cards don't lie!"

I stared blankly.

"It's true," she said. "There's no age limit on love."

"Shall we ask the cards about your gentleman friend?" I ventured clumsily.

"Friend?" she guffawed. "Why there's Mr. Fitch and Mr. Hayes and . . . ." As she continued through a list of half a dozen men, I found myself recalling a joke about an oldtimer contemplating the way he'd like to die— shot to death at the age of 94 by a jealous husband.

"But a retirement home must be like living in a fishbowl," I suggested.

"Naw," she laughed. "Nobody suspects old folks of having any interest. The few who know are too embarrassed to tell anyone else."

I hoped that one day I could be as carefree as Mrs. Abercrombie. We concluded the reading, which indicated she would have health and happiness for the next six months at least—I've found that six months is generally as far into the future as I can project. Then Mrs. Abercrombie was replaced by Mrs. Strick, a dour woman with a look of condensation in her eyes.

I was still basking in the glow of Mrs. Abercrombie's joie de vivre when Mrs. Strick interrupted my thoughts.

"Did she boast about her conquests?" she demanded.

"Who?"

"Virginia Abercrombie!"

"Well, I generally don't discuss readings with . . . ."

"You know how she does it, don't you, how she gets all the men?" It was obvious Mrs. Strick was going to tell me whether I wanted to know or not.

"She goes all the way!" Mrs. Strick spit the words at me.

God, I hope when I'm eighty, people say the same about me.

Mrs. Strick was not amused. I would read for Mrs. Abercrombie many times, but that would be my last reading for Mrs. Strick. I never saw her again.

Others I would read for only once, but for different reasons. One was Irene Portious, a nervous young woman in her late 20s. She had the look of one I would guess to be a skeptic rather than a seeker. But she had made an appointment and I was determined to read for her.

She fidgeted as I laid the cards on the table between us. She leaned forward, intently studying the spread. "Is there a Gemini, Libra or Aquarius man in your life," I asked. She jumped as if startled and sat upright. I looked into her face for some sign, but it was not her expression that caught my eye. There was movement immediately behind her.

There I saw the shape of a man, tall and thin. He wore dark slacks and a sport shirt, its sleeves rolled up to reveal pale, lean arms. His hair was dark.

It was as if I was looking at a double exposure. Through him I could see the furniture behind. But he was there, gazing down at me. I swallowed hard, unsure how to proceed.

At last, Miss Porteus answered.

"My brother in Vietnam."

"But he's not a soldier," I said, looking into the apparition.

"No," she said. "He was a teacher there, but he has

been missing for more than a year. My family believes he was with the CIA."

The face behind her turned away.

"Your brother is dead," I said. The head turned back to me and nodded. "He wants you to know that."

Miss Porteus covered her face and began to weep.

"I'm sorry," I began. "I didn't mean to . . . ."

"No," she assured me, "I'm relieved. Thank you. It's awful to live with the uncertainty. It's better to know the truth—or at least believe you know it."

I had broken my own rule—I had blurted out disastrous news without even considering the consequences. I had lost my composure in the face of one of those rare occurences that can shock even an experienced psychic. In the long run, I'm glad I did.

The spirit had disappeared. Miss Porteus did too at the conclusion of her reading. Later, she would write me a note saying if she ever felt the need for psychic help again, she would be in touch. That was the last I heard from her.

Reading for clients remained my first love but I was slowly expanding the outlets for my psychic energy. Two men for whom I read during that period would have a profound effect on how I would use those outlets. One was like an old friend the moment we ment. The other had seemed like a friend before we met but turned out to be something else entirely.

I had enjoyed entertainer Arte Johnson's work for a long time. He had been a regular on one of my favorite television shows, "Laugh-In," and I had been looking forward to meeting him since learning we would appear together on "Seattle Today."

"Seattle Today" remains one of the Puget Sound's favorite daytime TV programs. Its format is typical of the plethora of local talk shows throughout the country—what makes it unusual is the skill, the charm and the warmth of hosts Shirley Hudson and Cliff Lentz, who spend an hour each morning chatting with colorful local personalities and visiting celebrities.

Their producer, Milt Hughs, had called to invite me to make my first television appearance on their show. I was a veteran of the print medium, having been the subject of articles in newspapers and magazines, and had by now logged many hours on radio. But TV remained an exciting, new world for me.

The event became a family holiday. We allowed the children to skip school so they could watch me rub elbows with the stars. Mother and the children sat around our TV at home while I watched the show open on a monitor in KING TV's blue room and waited with Arte Johnson to be called to the set.

Arte seemed sympathetic when I told him it was to be my maiden voyage on the Seattle television air waves. It meant a lot to me to be appearing with a professional like him, I said. He smiled reassuringly and promised to help out any way he could.

To keep my hands busy, I read his cards and he professed to be impressed with the accuracy of the reading.

Then he was called and I was left to gnaw my fingernails for 15 minutes. At last, I too was ushered to the set.

Shirley and Cliff put me quickly at ease as I settled into a chair beside Arte. They kidded me goodnaturedly, asking if I actually believed in psychic phenomena. I admitted that yes, in fact, I was convinced that the mind had powers whose existence man had steadfastly denied throughout the ages.

"I'm not a fanatic, though," I explained. "I still have a lot of unanswered questions. But searching for the answers is fascinating."

Suddenly, without warning, the diminutive comedian, whose antics and observations had for so long delighted me, was chewing my legs off.

He launched into a diatribe against psychics in general and me in particular, saying the reading I had given earlier had been packed with gross generalities and misinformation. He concluded in a challenging tone.

"How much of what you say in a reading do you think is actually destined to happen?" he demanded. "And how much comes true because you plant the idea?"

"That's difficult to say," I admitted and recounted an amusing incident that had caused me to ponder that very question.

I had been having a recurring dream about a client being injured in a car accident involving a yellow Volkswagen. The time period of the impending disaster was very clear in my mind—the first two weeks in December—and so were the results. My friend was to suffer a broken leg. I was so convinced that I called to warn her about the impending disaster.

She claimed not to be persuaded. But to humor me and to be on the safe side, she decided to take a couple of weeks of vacation from Boeing and spend the days of doom at home.

The next time I saw her was the week following her vacation. She was on crutches.

"Oh, no!" I moaned.

She nodded forlornly. "You're not going to believe this," she began with a frown. Since Nana had the week off, she explained, her five-year-old grandson had come to keep her company. With him, he brought an armload of favorite toys.

She had stumbled across one of those toys while negotiating the stairs in the subdued light of morning, December 7. Her bumpy descent had ended with a fractured ankle.

"There I was in mortal pain, cursing my luck and your stupid prediction," she recalled. "Then I looked over to see what I had stepped on. It was a toy car—a little yellow Volkswagen."

I could feel the mood of the audience shift from one of affection for the television personality to one of resentment as he interrupted my story again and again with sarcastic comments. It was unnecessary for me to defend myself—the audience was responding with audible comments. Even Shirley and Cliff were coming to my defense.

Arte was backtracking with clever voices when the producer slipped a message to Shirley and she in turn leaned in my direction. Softly she asked if it would be all right to flash my home phone number on the screen—the studio switchboard was being jammed with calls.

I nodded and scribbled the number on a pad. In a few moments more, the show ended. Calmly, I shook Arte's hand and told him he had made my first television appearance a memorable one. I thanked Shirley and Cliff for inviting me, then walked quickly out of the studio.

Several hours and a few soothing drinks later, I arrived home to find Mother looking like she'd just been run over by a Bell telephone truck. The phone started ringing as soon as they flashed the number, she complained, and it has been ringing ever since. In fact, it would continue ringing for two more days; we received nearly 500 calls, many from viewers with a compulsion to apologize for Arte's borish behavior, but most from people interested in private readings.

The calls made me feel better about my first appearance on television—but not enough for me to cancel a vow never again to set foot in front of a camera. Nor was I spiritual enough to forgive and forget Arte.

It was several months later that the wounds were reopened when my sister brought me a copy of *National Enquirer*, a publication which has given vast publicity to psychic phenomena, but one I have tended to avoid for personal reasons. What had caught her eye was an interview with Arte Johnson.

Arte had finally admitted publicly that he believes in astrology. The turning point, he said, had been a very personal experience. He had been having a recurring dream in which a friend was injured in an accident involving a blue Mercedes.

The date of the accident and the fact that the friend

would suffer a broken leg had been revealed in the dream, he said. Arte admitted that at the time he doubted the likelihood such a prognostication could possibly come true. Yet he talked his friend into playing it safe by staying home.

A few days later, he saw the friend on crutches. And low and behold, when Arte asked what happened, the friend explained that while hiding out at home, he stepped on a toy car—a blue Mercedes, to be exact—and broke his leg.

I might have taken the disaster that befell Arte's friend personally if it hadn't been for the other man who had entered my life about the same time.

Bob Ranjel is a sensitive, soft-spoken man who convinced me that Arte Johnson was a teacher, sent expressly to reveal great truths.

"What did you learn from the experience?" he asked.

"That Arte Johnson is a real creep."

"And?"

"That the bigger they are—even if they're only five feet tall—the worse they can hurt you."

"Is that all?"

"I guess I learned what it feels like to be victimized."

"That's the important thing. You would never intentionally do what he did. But do you know for sure what he did, he did intentionally?"

I wanted to rip Bob's tongue out and thrash him with it. What was really irritating was that the longer I thought about it the more I realized that I had periodically trod dangerously close to humiliating others without realizing it.

"Who was the real loser in your exchange?" Bob asked with finality.

I didn't have to answer.

The balance with which he studies an issue before reaching a conclusion is one of Bob's outstanding qualities. But he has others that are equally aggravating. Like always giving advice that turns out to be good.

He has been giving me advice ever since we first met

in March 1974. Bob also introduced me to new levels of spiritualism, though I would be pulling your leg if I told you the initial attraction was entirely spiritual.

John Davis had called one spring Sunday to ask if he could bring his mother by for a reading. It was her birthday, he explained, and this was the gift she wanted.

Though I normally avoid working on weekends, I didn't have anything planned and so consented.

"Oh, and would you mind if I brought along a man who lives in the apartment next to mine?" John added. "He's heard a lot about you and would like a reading as well."

The problem with doing favors is that they tend to get out of hand. But two readings wouldn't take much longer than one, I reasoned, and it might be nice to have company for the afternoon.

"Sure," I said, "bring him along."

I guess it would be accurate to describe my first reaction as lust rather than love at first sight. Half-Spanish and half-French, Bob was every inch the tall, dark, handsome stranger I had been reading about in romance novels since the age of 12. But there was something familiar in the look that passed between us as he entered the door.

Both of us felt it instantly—we had known one another before.

His reading turned into one of the longest I have ever given. Over and over I spread the cards, wanting them to tell me everything about this man.

He was a Taurus, had been victimized by ethnic prejudice in his childhood, had withdrawn and was now finding his way out once more. We talked for what seemed like hours while Mother entertained my other guests.

Then I did a spread I rarely attempt. I had discovered it in a text called *The Devil's Picturebook*—which is not nearly as ominous as it sounds.

Sometimes, using this 12-card spread as a focal point,

I have been able to scan past lives of those for whom I am reading. I don't see entire lives, just glimpses, like sepia tone film clips.

It seems that everyone else who ever mastered this technique has found among his clients the rich, the well-born and the able of past ages—everyone from Napoleon to Sitting Bull. I have never been so fortunate. The closest I ever came was a client who was Pope for less than a month before someone poisoned him in the 16th century. For the most part, those I have done past life readings for were simple souls, primarily soldiers or peasants, the victims of the famous and the infamous.

I avoided giving such readings for two reasons. First, I saw no real value in them—how could it possibly improve your life as a housewife, to know you were once Queen of Sheba? But equally inhibiting was the fact that this technique leaves me exhausted. When I have completed the 12-card spread, I'm so physically and mentally depleted that it's impossible to drag myself out of bed the next day.

I did a 12-card spread for Bob because I was curious whether we had known one another in some previous life.

We had. But seldom as lovers.

In the late 1880s, he was a British doctor whose drunken neglect led to my death. I was not totally without blame in the incident, though. His love affair with spiritualism in a liquid form had reduced him to the role of abortionist. That's why I had gone to see him.

In an earlier life, we had lived in the Mideast, where we had an illicit relationship which led to our flight into the desert. There we ran out of water and became lost. For days we suffered before he put me out of my misery.

He showed a real talent for expediting my demise. I found only one lifetime we shared in which he didn't do me in. We were teachers together in an ancient civilization. I don't recall many details, though. I had allowed myself to become preoccupied with the recurring death scenes.

I could barely keep my eyes open by the time the reading concluded but I was conscious enough to hear Bob's invitation to dinner and theater next weekend, and to wonder if based on our past lives together, I might be better off washing my hair instead.

I decided to take a chance. And when that one proved painless, I took another, then another until finally I took the biggest chance of all—marriage. My life and my family would be whole once more.

I sometimes think Bob was fated to marry me in this lifetime as penance for the shabby way he treated me in past lives. If that is the case, he has born his penance with patience and paid for his sins a thousand times over.

Perhaps as retribution for the sloppy abortion, he has become father-figure to my children. He is there when they need him, dispensing justice and gentle encouragement, giving of himself more than most natural fathers.

Like Mother, Bob is a well that never seems to run dry, one that I drink from as greedily as anyone in the family. It was Bob who helped awaken my spiritualism and revealed the importance of past lives. But first, he helped me grapple with more worldly concerns.

I might still be adhering to my vow to avoid the media if Bob hadn't convinced me to come back out of the closet. (Did he really convince me or did he force me to convince myself?)

"What are you afraid of?" he asked one day. His voice was soft and seductive.

"Looking foolish," I answered testily.

"You look foolish when you refuse the challenge," he said. For a moment, I thought he was going to call me "Grasshopper."

We debated the issue for days. I would spill forth the anguish of my soul, the uncertainty, the pain, the emotion. He would counter with cool, clear logic just to irritate me. At last he began fighting dirty.

"I'm glad you've decided to stay at home," he said. "I don't think it's what you're meant to do but if it makes you happy, it makes all of us happy. It's good to have you right here where you belong."

I knew it was child psychology. I knew he was appealing to my contrary nature. But I couldn't help myself. Within a matter of days, I was responding to invitations to appear on radio and television talk shows.

During the odyssey of my youth, I had sung in nightclubs. I had enjoyed entertaining but had doubted that I had either the talent or the tenacity to make a career of it. Now I was finding an outlet for that old urge to perform and a new urge to respond to detractors. Radio talk show hosts love controversies which will tweek the interest of their listeners, and psychic phenomena is one of the most controversial subjects in any market.

With my evangelistic juices flowing, I would sit behind the microphone explaining that I was not anti-Christ. In fact, I am a devout Christian. But I also am devout in my belief in the paranormal, at least that portion I have been fortunate enough to witness. That was all it took for the religious conservatives to begin heating up the phone lines, to proselytize, to quote scripture, to damn and to cajole.

I was amazed that I seldom had to defend myself for long. Members of less conservative religions were soon on the line, responding to the allegations against me and other psychics, encouraging a serious consideration of the subject, ridiculing claims that religion and extrasensory perception were in conflict. The faith of these callers gave me faith and a determination to find other outlets for reaching audiences.

It was in 1977 that George McDermont, a local advertising executive and one of my favorite clients, found one. He had hatched a scheme that would put me and several of my colleagues on center stage.

Among George's major clients was a restaurant called Latitude 47. It was a lovely restaurant with excellent food and a wealth of atmosphere. George had come up with a slogan that captured the flavor of the place—"Come to your senses at Latitude 47."

It offered sights, sounds, smells, tastes and physical comfort, the advertisement explained.

So why not add a sixth sense? George reasoned.

He talked the manager into introducing a unique brand of entertainment—psychics. There were five of us in all.

I read tarot cards. Barb Easton, who was to become my closest friend, read spreads of a conventional deck, and Judith Ballard, another close friend, was graphologist. Palmist Eva Spatheth and numerologist John Davis completed the ensemble.

We were paid by the house to circulate among customers performing our specialties at no charge. We worked together for nearly a year before we decided that despite the exposure we were getting, the salary just wasn't worth the time and effort we had to invest.

Barb and I broke away. We appeared on "Seattle Today" and several radio shows together, then set off on our own to match the fame we were generating with a bigger share of the fortune.

Barb and I are kindred souls, vagabonds in a gypsy profession. But unlike me, she had come to it not so much by necessity, as by choice. She had decided to step down as a $35,000 a year executive for a jewelry firm to explore this strange gift she had discovered she possessed.

At first her employer had refuse to accept her resignation. She was having a breakdown, her bosses agreed. But she was adamant.

"I quit," she emphatically assured them.

We had known one another less than a month when she became the psychic I turned to for readings. Like most psychics, I find it impossible to read for myself. So Barb read for me. It normally isn't a good idea to have your closest friend read for you—she can be as subjective as you are and reading cards demands objectivity.

Barb has never had difficulty mustering objectivity in reading my cards, however. In fact, I sometimes think she takes delight in being brutally candid with me.

"You're going to have severe problems with the new house," she said one day as she studied a spread of cards. Bob and I were in the process of building on a wooded acreage we had scrimped and saved to buy.

"What to you mean?" I demanded.

"I don't know," she answered. "I just feel that the project is heading for disaster."

"What am I going to do? Every dime we own is tied up in that house. Are we going to lose it?"

"You, of all people, should know the cards don't tell everything," Barb replied, "but if you'd like, I can make up some details for you."

Barb and I began offering restaurants a unique deal—entertainment they didn't have to pay for. All they had to do was advertise our appearance and pick up the tab for our dinner and drinks. We took care of the rest, charging customers $5 for each reading.

Everyone except Barb and I expected the venture to fail. Our clairvoyance proved accurate. Customers would make reservations for readings as soon as they entered the restaurant and within the first half hour, we generally were booked for the remainder of the evening. The restaurateurs loved us—customers would finish dinner, find out they still had an hour to kill before their reading and adjourn to the cocktail lounge to wait.

We soon had a following, a band of regulars who would show up wherever we were reading. We also had restaurant owners bidding for our time.

Barb and I began mixing business with pleasure, taking periodic bookings in areas of the Northwest in which we wanted to spend a week or two vacationing. The fall they put the finishing touches on my new home, Bob and Barb talked me into an engagement in a city in Alaska. The strain of work and rushing to complete the house before winter were taking their toll—I had become as much fun as an icewater bath.

But our Alaska outing would not be the most relaxing two weeks Barb and I ever spent.

I won't name the city—I may have to go back there someday. But it was one of Alaska's largest.

We went there in the off season, a good time for vacationing if you want to economize. My sister, Jacquie, who works for a major airline, booked us accommodations she described as modest. I described them as archaic when I discovered they sold beer by the case in the lobby. I christened the facility the Fault Line Hotel.

We were given a corner suite on the fourth floor. To the best of our knowledge, we were the only tenants at that level. In fact, we were convinced we were the only guests in the entire hotel.

The door to the suite opened onto a short hallway. To the left was a bathroom, then a kitchenette, which opened onto what we laughingly referred to as a sitting room, complete with a hide-a-bed. Beyond the sitting room was a single bedroom.

I staked claim to the bedroom since I was the first one into the suite. That left Barb to take up residence in the sitting room, which was about as wide as a boxcar and nearly as comfortable.

"He'd be a real hunk if it weren't so strange," Barbara said after the hotel's Jack-of-all-trades—blonde, blue-eyed Phil Burton—accepted a 50-cent tip for carrying our bags and left us to explore our temporary quarters. Phil was about 18, broad-shouldered, athletic-looking. But an apparent birth defect had left him with a twisted mouth and a noticeable lisp.

"Did you notice his eyes?" I asked. "They're so big and innocent. A girl could get lost in there."

"Fortunately, neither of us is a girl," Barb mused. "This room really gives me the creeps."

She was right about the room. It was reasonably comfortable, despite its design, but there was something disconcerting about it. Perhaps it was the interminable silence. We couldn't even hear traffic on the street below.

"Let's get out of here," I suggested. We groped our way down the dimly lit hall—I estimated that none of the bulbs was larger than 30-watt—then waited a long time for the elevator.

When the door finally opened, Barb let out a shriek, which was answered by a shriek from within. I looked into the elevator to find an elderly couple huddled at the back of the compartment. The shock of seeing other humans in the hotel had been too much for Barb and the woman.

They babbled apologies as the elevator proceeded to the lobby, then Barb and I fled into the sunlight. Half a dozen Sangrias and a steak dinner later, we were back in our room watching a little prime-time television— "How to Lift a Moose."

It was nine o'clock when a knock at the door echoed like rifle fire through our cramped quarters.

Barb looked at me.

I looked at Barb.

"Gonna answer it?" she asked.

"Are you?"

Nervously, we tiptoed down the short hallway.

"Who is it?" I called.

"Phil Burton."

"Phil Burton," I whispered to Barb.

"Phil Burton," she agreed.

I waited to see if she was going to open the door. At last she shrugged and released the safety lock.

"Thought you might like some company," Phil said sheepishly.

"Sure," said Barb, "come on in."

Phil turned out to be a delightful conversationalist. He regaled us with his life story—the son of a Minnesota minister, he had dropped out of college and come to Alaska to find himself. He let us in on gossip about the hotel and warned against unsavory nightspots unescorted women should avoid. Barb and I made mental notes on the bars that sounded worth exploring.

It was well past midnight when Barb finally announced, "I'm tired. Go so I can get some sleep." We all laughed and Phil departed into the early morning darkness.

It was 10 o'clock the next morning when I awoke to the sound of Barb shuffling around in the sitting room. I crawled out of bed, stumbled into the room and plopped into a chair.

"Have you seen my ring?" Barb asked as she plunged her hand down the side of the cushion on which I was sitting. I knew immediately which ring she was talking about, a large, diamond cocktail ring she wore everywhere except to bed; apparently she was afraid of cutting her throat with it in her sleep.

"No," I answered. "Where did you leave it?"

"I left it on the end table," she cried, "but it's not there now."

We turned the room over twice, shaking out every piece of linen, pulling cushions from the furniture, scouring the carpeting. Then we called the desk.

Within minutes, Phil was at the door, armed with a vacuum cleaner and an armload of fresh linens. He tsk-tsked about the room, turning it over once more, shaking out bed clothes and replacing them with new ones, then vacuuming the floor and sifting through the bag to be sure the ring hadn't been sucked up inside.

It was fruitless. The ring had vanished.

Barb was beside herself. The ring, which was worth several thousand dollars, had tremendous sentimental value. It had been given her by someone she refused to identify, even to me.

She moped about for seven days, leaving me to wonder if perhaps she thought I had taken it. After all, we were the only ones in the room that night.

Fortunately, we kept busy enough that the subject came up only infrequently. We spent our days on television talk shows or reading for private clients who had heard we were in town. Our evenings were spent at the club. We usually finished off with a nightcap at one of the bars Phil had warned us against.

We saw Phil leaning against the building when we stopped back at the hotel Thursday afternoon to freshen up before our evening at the club. When he spotted us, he hurried in our direction.

"Guess what!" he lisped. "I'm getting married."

"Oh, that's wonderful, Phil," said Barb.

"When, Phil?" I asked enthusiastically.

"Next Saturday."

Like an excited child he gushed about how he had found the love of his life, a young woman named Vicki. She'd only been in town a few weeks and knew virtually no one except Phil. It had been love at first sight, he said. They had been living together and now she had consented to become his wife.

Barb and I were as delighted as if a favorite nephew had just announced his impending marriage. Phil had become our pet, the one bright spot in the gloomy Fault Line Hotel.

Barb and I chattered all night about the wedding, deciding we would put off our departure an extra day so we could attend. We would want to buy the happy couple a gift. But what should it be? And what could you buy for newlyweds in this God-forsaken place?

We set out early the next morning to find out, but were stopped dead in our tracks by the sight of Phil slumped in a chair in the lobby. His eyes were red and swollen, as if he'd been crying.

"Are you all right?" Barb asked.

"No," he answered, his voice cracking. "It's Vicki. She's in the hospital. She got run over by a hit-and-run driver last night."

"My God," I said, "that's terrible."

"The wedding will have to be postponed, of course," Phil croaked. "I don't know what I'm going to do."

Barb and I comforted him as best we could, then left in a daze.

"How could something like this happen?" I wondered aloud.

"We really should stop by and see her," Barb suggested. "She doesn't know anyone in town and it might make her feel a little better."

"Good idea," I agreed.

We bought a bouquet of roses and caught a cab to the hospital, a monolithic structure overlooking the city.

It didn't dawn on us till we got there that we didn't know Vicki's last name.

"We're looking for a young woman named Vicki," Barb told the woman at the desk.

"What's her last name?"

"We don't know."

"Well, I can't very well look through every patient's card for a Vicki."

"Well, this woman was a hit-and-run victim who was brought in last night."

"Oh, you're talking about the attempted murder."

"Attempted murder?"

"Another one of the women some maniac has been driving over."

"I'm not sure I understand," said Barb.

"You haven't heard?"

"We're new in town," I explained.

"You're the psychics, aren't you?" she asked. She had seen us on one of the television talk shows, she explained.

Recognition is so fulfilling, especially when it helps cut through red tape.

"We're looking for the fiancee of a friend of ours," I told her. "He said she had been hit by a car and was a patient here."

"Well, the only patient we have who was hit by a car is a Dorthy Melton."

"Can we see her?" Barb asked.

The nurse brought us to a room in which a beautifully constructed brunette with a face that looked like it had gone through a meat grinder lay bound in bandages.

"Are you Vicki?" I asked.

"That's my stage name."

"Stage name?"

"I'm a dancer at the Liberty Lounge."

"Liberty Lounge," I blurted, recalling the list of places Phil had warned us to stay clear of. "That's a topless, bottomless bar!" Barb discreetly bruised three of my ribs with her elbow. The expression on her face told me she was as perplexed as I was.

"We were sorry to hear about your accident," Barb began.

"It was no accident," Vicki declared. "Someone tried to kill me."

"We're friends of your fiance," Barb continued undaunted. "We understand you're new in town and just wanted to stop by and see if there is anything we could do."

"Fiance? If I had a fiance, do you think I'd be dancing naked in a bar?"

"Phil Burton. . . ?"

"Filbert? Yes, I know crazy Phil. He dances at the club, but he's not my fiance. I barely know him, just to say "Hi" is all. Hell, he's queer as a three-dollar bill."

So much for psychic insights.

Barb and I left the hospital at a dead run.

We spent the afternoon in a nearby bar, where we were joined by an investigative reporter we had met at the newspaper. We told her about Phil Burton and she told us about "Hot Wheels," the name the news media had given a slayer who had been taking young women into the high country, beating them senseless, and running over them with his car until they were mutilated far past the point of death.

He had brought his act into the city three months before and in the interim had run over five more women. The longer we talked, the clearer it became that Phil Burton wasn't as harmless as he had looked. Chances were, he was a flaming fruitcake.

We drove with the reporter to the police station, where we described the more than coincidental relationship between details Phil had told us about himself

and what was known about the Hot Wheels slayings—
the fact that Phil had been at a resort at the same time
one of the murders occurred there, for instance. Then
we described discrepancies in how he and Vicki saw
their relationship.

Almost as an afterthought, Barb mentioned the
missing ring. We stood looking at one another in a state
of shock: had Phil come back into our suite while we
slept, we wondered? I felt a little queasy.

The police said they'd be in touch.

Barb and I slunk back into the hotel late that night,
certain that at every turn we were going to run into
Phil. But he was nowhere to be seen.

Once in our suite, I cautiously checked out the closets
while Barb gerryrigged an alarm system, setting the
coffee table just inside the door and stacking it precar-
iously with pots and pans.

Barb armed herself with the only sharp knife in the
house and I carried an iron skillet into my bedroom to
keep me company.

"You don't want to change beds tonight, do you?"
Barb suggested.

"Not on your life," I answered.

"Some friend you are; if he breaks in, I'm as good as
dead."

"Yes, but that would be a blessing. The phone's out
here—there's no way I could call for help. Can you
imagine how horrible it would be for me, lying in my
warm bed listening to one of the dearest people on earth
being snuffed and knowing I could be next?"

Barb thought about it a while.

"Why is it that gives me so little comfort?" she asked
at last.

Neither of us slept that night. The building which
had previously seemed so silent was now a symphony
of noises, creaks, bumps and bangs.

"You look like you slept with your eyes in an ink-
well," Barb said the next morning as I dragged myself
into the sitting room.

"Thank you," I said, "and you certainly look lovely today."

We occupied ourselves with rude remarks until a rap at the door silenced us. For a moment we stood motionless. Then I bolted for the bathroom door.

"I think it's for you," I called over my shoulder as I crashed into our burglar alarm, spreading a wave of clanging pots and pans cascading down the hall.

I slammed the bathroom door behind me, locked it and pressed my full weight against it. I could feel my heart pounding like an engine in urgent need of a tune-up.

"Who is it?" I heard Barb call in a meek voice.

"Police," the deep voice on the other side of the door answered without a trace of a lisp.

Tentatively, I unlocked the bathroom door and peeked out to watch Barb tentatively unlocking the door to the hall. Then she jumped back, nearly stumbling over a large pan as she admitted an ugly little policeman who was the most beautiful sight I had ever seen.

He paused long enough to plot a course through the wasteland of cooking utensils, then stepped gingerly into the sitting room.

"The captain asked me to stop by and tell you ladies not to worry about your little friend," he was saying as I approached from the bathroom. "He has been taken care of," he added with finality.

Barb offered him a seat but he shook his head.

"Which one lost the ring?"

"I did," said Barb.

"Well, the detectives think they might have a pretty good idea where it went but it will be a couple of weeks before they have a chance to check out all the leads. We'll need your address and phone number so we can reach you if it turns up."

Barb and I hugged one another and giggled with relief when the policeman had gone. Then we went back to bed. For the next several days, were checked every issue of the newspaper for stories on Phil Burton's arrest but never saw one. We called our investigative reporter friend, but she was on assignment somewhere up on the Alaska pipeline. No one else seemed to have any idea what we were talking about.

Winter set in shortly after we returned to Seattle. Winter in the Northwest is overcast. It rarely snows in places like Seattle, but it rains incessantly. Bob and I had beaten the rain, moving into the new house days before the first torrential downpour.

It wasn't the Lakebay estate, but our new home was spacious, comfortable and quiet. Only one neighboring house was visible from ours. Otherwise, the view was entirely one of trees, streams and wildflowers.

The house was split level, with a large living room, formal dining room and kitchen on the upper floor. Down the hall were Mother's bedroom and bath, and the master bedroom, complete with its own jacuzzi. Below was my office and sitting room, a family room, utility room and a bedroom for each of the children. I had spent hours decorating our new home. Unfortunately, I had failed to determine if it was seaworthy before we moved in.

The first rain brought with it a flood to rival Noah's. The downstairs was under four feet of water and so was all the furniture. We bailed and pumped and loaded up the moving van and headed back to Eunice's house. Now I was positive I was cursed—Eunice refused to let me go. It is crazy, I know, but that's the way I was beginning to feel. Our builder left town with $6,000 of our money. We filed suit, then our attorney left town with the depositions in his case.

"Someone has a Shirlee Teabo voodoo doll and is poking it full of needles," I raved.

Bob smiled with understanding and shook his head sadly.

"Into every life a little rain must fall," Barb said with a philosophical smile.

"You've got to be kidding me!" I screamed.

My husband, the man Ruth Montgomery has called

the most spiritual man she has ever met, helped me turn the energy of my anger and frustration inward and put it to productive use. We began to explore past lives together. The experience proved a catharsis for me.

"Our past lives are important to the present," said Bob, an accomplished hypnotherapist specializing in past life regressions. "Most of us have lived before and what we learned we carry with us. Those lessons are important to us now. But just as important is an understanding of the source of those lessons and the debts we have accrued in gaining them."

Bob helped open the passageway to the Akashic Record, a chronicle of past lives since the beginning of time, and with Xan as my guide I spent days looking at the ancestry of everyone I knew.

It was fascinating to see a familiar face dissolve into an earlier manifestation only to dissolve once more to an even earlier one. Often the person's sex changed from lifetime to lifetime. There were common characteristics in the face from one of its mortal generations to the next, so that as I watched its reverse evolution unfold, it was like watching a single face in transition. yet I was startled to realize how little similarity there was between the faces at the extremes of this process.

I was intrigued by the perspective my glimpses of past lives gave to my understanding of history. I had been raised on Cecil B. DeMille's technicolor view of our heritage. It turned out that history wasn't nearly so colorful nor so grand as it had been depicted on the silver screen.

It was a long time before I realized the shabby horde behind which trailed carts of ragged women and children was the proud Roman army. The brightest color I saw was a reddish-brown tunic worn by an officer who was greeted by bows when he strode through the ranks. I was a peasant on the fringes of the spectacle and recall that when I humbled myself before my betters, I found myself looking at the bare backside of the equally humble soldier in front of me. So much for the glory that was Rome.

For years I had wondered about a seemingly insurmountable compulsion to eat. Not that I'm attracted to junk food, mind you. I'm obsessed by good food and good drink and lots of it, a fact which has resulted in my losing the same 20 pounds 100 times in my present lifetime.

I found the explanation in the Akashic Record, along with an insight into why I never allowed myself to hunch over like most other tall teenage women. Though I stand nearly six feet tall, I have never slumped, never attempted to hide my height.

In a shabby little castle somewhere in antiquity I found myself a hunchbacked dwarf waiting on a straw-covered floor for the master's banquet to be served. I wasn't a pleasant hunchback, a court jester. No such luck. I was an anxious, hateful little man. Rather than make others laugh, I kept them from death. I was a food taster, sipping and sampling everything that would be served on the master's table. I didn't get big bites, just enough to make sure it wasn't lethal. Then off the banquet went.

I was left to hurry back to the servants quarters, where the poor meal that was being served would invariably have been gobbled up in my absence. I was forever hungry, forever resentful.

It was nice to know I was at least progressing in stature. I also discovered that through the ages, I have been progressing toward an understanding of the psychic world. I saw the earliest roots of my gift take hold and begin to grow. I saw the first fruit passed from generation to generation, ripening as it went. Talents I had assumed everyone was born with I found had to develop through lifetimes. The capacity to speak to and understand animals, for instance. I saw an age when that feat was impossible for me and another in which it would have cost me my life.

The experience converted me. From disinterest in

past lives, I have become an exponent of the virtues of knowing where we have been so we will have a better awareness of where we are going.

In early February, Barb got a call from Alaska. The police had located her missing ring. She left on a Friday morning to pick it up. Late that night she called. She was so furious she could barely speak.

"What's the matter?" I demanded. "Didn't they have the ring?"

"They had it. Some guy with a lisp pawned it."

"Then what's wrong?"

"It's Phil. Do you know where he is?"

"In a rubber room, I hope."

"He's in California."

"California," I yelped. "Did he escape?"

"One of the policemen gives me back my ring and I ask, 'What about Phil, have you got a case against him?' He says, 'Naw, we just ran the little creep out of town.'"

"Do we have a bad connection?" I shouted. "Did you say they ran him out of town?"

"That's what I said. I said, 'You did what?' He says, 'We ran him out of town. Said he had a job lined up as a male nurse down in California so we sent him packing.' Then he says, 'He should fit in real fine down there.'"

"They actually let him get away?" I was incredulous.

"Look, lady, this is Alaska," Barb said in her best official police impersonation. "It's like the last frontier. We have different values up here. We don't take some things as seriously as you folks do down in the lower 48."

"Like murder?"

"That's what he said. He said, 'We're rid of him and that's all that matters now.'"

I looked for Phil Burton in the Akashic Record but found no trace of him. I look for him in the newspaper every day, half expecting to see that a male nurse with a noticeable lisp has been captured after wrecking havoc on some sundrenched metropolitan center. Maybe they didn't really run him out of town; maybe he's holding up the trunk of some future woodland giant.

I'm curious. But not curious enough to press the issue.

I find myself seeking those familiar blue eyes as Bob and I continue to explore spiritual planes, levels to which souls gravitate after death. There are planes on which life goes on just as it does on earth, where souls unequipped to deal with the reality of death exist in an earth-like twilight zone complete with streets and houses and old friends until called upon to return once more to the living.

In stages, souls seem to work themselves free of earth's attraction, growing more spiritual from age to age, lifetime to lifetime. Eventually, they graduate through realms of higher existence until they enter a realm of pure energy and pure intellect unfettered by time or space.

It is here they not only reach out their hands to touch the face of God but become one with his spirit. Even a soul as troubled as Phil Burton's can aspire to such heights and attain them.

Heresy, you say?

I think not.

CHAPTER 10

I didn't recall having turned on the tape recorder. But a full half hour of tape had wound through the machine sometime during the night. And when I played it back, the voice was unmistakably my own, though measured, distant and eerie.

My sister Jacquie had been researching the question of whether dolphins communicate with one another, not only through sound but by means of telepathy as well. It is an intriguing question.

On a purely gut level, I believe they do—perhaps because I want to believe in their ability to communicate. Those who see sacrilege in my belief in past lives will be doubly offended by my faith that there are other reasoning animals on earth than man.

There exists between man and sea mammals such as dolphins a strange, special affinity; it is one of curiosity, affection and kinship. Their sense of play touches our hearts. We observe them solving problems, yes, even reasoning—not just reacting. Their attempt at friendship and communication with man, that aura of wisdom, touches our souls.

Legends involving the affinity between man and dolphins have been with us for eons. Prehistoric tableaus depicting these sea animals frolicking with ancient man have been unearthed in South Africa. The theme has recurred in art form in Etruscan, Greek and Roman ruins. But until the past few years, such interaction has been generally dismissed as myth or wishful thinking. Research that demonstrated that dolphins were able to communicate with one another—seemingly in complete thoughts—raised questions for which science had no ready answers.

Yet the possibility that man was not the only rational animal on earth was too tantalizing to pass up.

Dolphins, it was noted, have a brain nearly the same size as that of man. But more surprising was the similarity in the interconnection between the two hemispheres of the human and dolphin brains and the fact that their cellular densities and connections are as large and complex as our own. In short, there seemed to be evidence that dolphins might be as capable of abstract thought as are humans.

Jacques Cousteau says in *Dolphins*, "The dolphin brain is capable of memory, of associating ideas." If only they could communicate to man their memories, their history and their secrets of survival over 30 million years.

A handful of scientists began taking seriously such ancient tales as Aristotle's description of dolphins raising their heads above water in an apparent   effort to imitate human sounds.

"On two or three occasions, we looked at each other," Cousteau said, "and their eyes sparkled with an expected gleam of connivance, as though the most intelligent of the dolphins was about to reveal, at last, the great secret which would permit man finally to cross over the chasm separating humanity from animality, finally to restore to life its primordial unity."

Many researchers believe this unity is possible; that sea mammals respond to seemingly silent signals among themselves. More startling though are "off the record" accounts which seem to indicate that telepathic communication may be possible between man and the minions of the sea.

Dr. John Lilly, who heads the Human/Dolphin Research Foundation at Malibu, California, explains why serious scientists have difficulty discussing such incidents publicly. "A certain willingness to face censure, to be a maverick, to question one's beliefs, to revise them, is obviously necessary," Lilly said in the fifth annual Lasker Lecture at Michael Reese Hospital and Medical Center in Chicago. "But what is not obvious is how to prepare one's own mind to receive the transmissions from the far side of the protective, transparent wall separating each of us from the dark gulf of the unknown. Maybe we must realize that we are still babies in the universe, taking steps never before taken. Sopmetimes we reach out from our aloneness for someone else who may or may not exist. But at least, we reach out, and it is gratifying to see our dolphins reach also, however primitively. They reach toward those of us who are willing to reach toward them. It may be that someday not too far distant we both can draw to an end the 'long loneliness'. . . ."

Lilly delivered his lecture in 1962 but progress since then has remained slow. And most scientists have remained timid. Privately, they admit to being intrigued by the possibility that lines of communication might eventually be opened.

They encourage serious research and pledge their support and expertise. But for the time being, they feel compelled to maintain their anonymity—they have their professional reputations to protect.

I sympathize with their dilemma and respect their need to stay out of the limelight. For many years, I kept secret the fact that I talked to animals. I didn't want to be branded a nut. And I didn't even have a professional reputation to protect.

When I finally shared my secret, I was surprised to learn that nearly every other animal lover I knew had remarkably similar incidents to tell, times when a jubilant mood had been shattered into depression by momentary eye contact with an otherwise seemingly contented animal.

I didn't find my sister's research particularly shocking, but was intrigued by the range of intelligence scientists have come to believe dolphins possess.

One man who believes is Frank Robson. Recipient of the 1974 Gold Medal from the Netherlands government, he is considered one of the leading dolphin trainers and researchers in the world. Robson's first contact with dolphins was as a fisherman off the coast of New Zealand. Through his daily dealing with dolphins he became convinced they could be communicated with by thought. He devised a method for painless capture of dolphins, then demonstrated successfully his thought-training technique for the directors on Napier Marineland in New Zealand. Until his resignation as Marineland's Head Trainer, neither the shrill demand of whistles nor the rewards of fish were used there. Yet, six trained dolphins performed fetes requiring split second timing and complicated series of tasks guided entirely by the thoughts of the trainer. In Robson's excellent book, *Thinking Dolphins, Talking Whales*, he describes how he accomplished it. "I started training at Marineland convinced that a dolphin trainer can transfer his thoughts to the animal and receive back its thoughts in return," he said. "That to do so he must free himself from his preoccupation with language and start to think actions and feelings rather than words. For words, after all, only describe actions and feelings." It is this transfer of feelings and emotions that make the man and dolphin relationship unique. We seem to be each looking for something from the other. But we are not certain what that something is.

Robson has noticed that although up to 190,000 people visit Napier Marineland each year, the dolphins respond to the presence of certain individuals—they can pick them out of the crowd. In one instance, they stopped a performance, hurried to the edge of the pool and followed the movements of a young woman wherever she went. Robson was as perplexed as the woman by the behavior. Later he removed her from the dolphins' line of vision, then took her off the premises. He was amazed to observe that the dolphins seemed to keep track of her, becoming noticeably exicited when she approached through the gates unseen by them. The dolphins could determine when and from what direction she would come, Robson said, adding that similar incidents occur two or three times a year. "The only constant seems to be that the person in question is a true animal lover," says Robson. "I am certain it will eventually be accepted that dolphins are able to receive instant, unspoken communication from certain humans and that such people, in many cases, transmit this communication without knowing it." There are other incidents of sea-going mammals responding to man's thoughts and directions, from television stars like Flipper to Namu the Killer Whale. In a sense, they are not really trained, but are participating and cooperating by choice.

True communication is a two-way process, however; we must learn to listen to their messages. Many such attempts to understand their "language" already are underway.

One such attempt is called project JANUS. "The brain of the JANUS is the computer with two sets of inputs and outputs, one set for man; the other for dolphin," Dr. Lilly explained. This project is a major scientific endeavor in which listening to the messages of the dolphin on their terms is the priority.

There is widespread belief among researchers, including Dr. Lilly, that if we can learn to communicate with dolphins, we can learn to communicate with extraterrestrial beings if it ever becomes necessary.

I believe outer space and inner space—both of the planet and of man—are integrally related. Perhaps the intelligent beings of the sea are the link to understanding that connection. I meant to see for myself.

Jacquie made several calls on my behalf and in every instance found researchers willing to take me out on Puget Sound to attempt to "talk" with the orcas or to teach me scuba diving techniques so I could enter pools with captive dolphins.

Plans were being formalized for my first date with a dolphin, when I found the used tape in my recorder.

I keep the recorder on my bedstand to enable me to tape thoughts or dreams that occur to me during the night. It has proven an invaluable tool since like most people, I have a terrible time remembering nocturnal revelations over breakfast the next morning.

But I don't ever recall having recorded without at least remembering turning on the machine. And to the best of my knowledge I've never used the words or the tone that appeared on this tape.

My voice occupies only a couple of moments on the half-hour tape. It is distant, barely audible unless the volume is turned to near maximum. What the message means, I can only speculate. But I know it haunts me, luring me in new directions. I leave it to you to draw your own conclusions.

"When the Gods divided the land and the sea, two civilizations blossomed. The ones of the land became warlike and destructive, and the Old Ones were angry. The ones of the sea developed and grew. And as it came time for the revisit, the Old Ones were pleased.

"Our water brothers developed into kind, divine souls, with technology far beyond the earth people. Never once have they been warlike or denied help and succor when our land masses fell.

"And even now we invade their home, their power source, as cannibals.

"As the Gods and Elders revisit here, so do they sit in counsel with those under the waters. It's only because of their caring and their patience that we have not been destroyed.

"The time is now, the time is here for the meeting. And that which is seen and that which is unseen merge into the whole."

CHAPTER 11

Things that go bump in the night are seldom the ghosts we expect them to be. Usually they are nothing more than a loose shutter or a rafter that hasn't quite settled into place.

But with alarming regularity, they turn out to be the unwitting work of a frustrated teenager, according to Judith Ballard. My friend Judith is a versatile, multi-talented psychic who for the past twenty years has, among other things, been hunting ghosts and dehaunting houses.

Most dictionaries consider ghost and poltergeist synonymous terms, but Judith draws a distinction between the two. Ghosts are exactly what you'd expect them to be, she says—they're spirits of once-living humans. But poltergeists are something else entirely.

"There are two types of poltergeist," Judith explained over lunch one day. "The rarest is the mischievous spirit that has never taken human form. These manifestations are known in various cultures by such names as elves, gremlins and leprechauns."

Far more common but far less understood is the poltergeist Judith described as random energy, usually expelled by an emotionally troubled teenager. Typically, this can be the source of such phenomena as dishes mysteriously hurling themselves across a room or books tumbling from shelves.

Or spontaneous fires, I thought, recalling Xanthea

and the incredible self-starting drapes and bed clothes.
Where had Judith been when I was young and naive
and needed her most, I wondered. It had been several
years after Xanthea had stopped subconsciously trying
to burn down the house that I first met Judith.

We had worked together a number of times since, the
most memorable experience following shortly on the
heels of the discovery of the skull of a mutual acquain-
tance who had disappeared a year earlier. That was the
time I singlehandedly set psychic research back a couple of centuries by responding to a telephone inter-
viewer who asked if I had reached any conclusions in
the case.

"There are strong indications that she was the victim
of foul play," I answered. It took little psychic ability to
draw that conclusion since the skull had been found
partially buried in an abandoned field.

Judith was more circumspect. Through psychometry
she reached a number of conclusions police believed
were accurate. They fit perfectly into the theory police
had formulated. Unfortunately, police could never
come up with the clue they needed to prove their theory
correct—at least not in a court of law.

And so another criminal remains free.

I realized that at the moment Judith was explaining
that dishes and tumbling books were the symptoms
described by a woman who had called soliciting her
psychic assistance a couple of years earlier. The woman
was convinced she had a ghost and would need Judith's
help in exorcising it. But Judith was dubious.

"Do you have an adolescent who's going through
puberty?" Judith asked.

"Yes," the woman replied, obviously perplexed by the
question. She had a teenage son, she said.

Though the woman denied that her son was unhappy,
she admitted that the mysterious incidents had begun
shortly after he visited her estranged husband.

Judith wasn't surprised that the boy denied any
unhappiness. "The kind of phenomenon we're discuss-

ing occurs when a teenager is experiencing chemical changes in the body," she says. "These changes combine with emotional upheaval to disturb the child's psychic balance." Parapsychologists have found that fear, guilt, frustration or anger the adolescent is feeling can cause an energy that creates sometimes-violent disturbances.

"In a few, very rare instances, a child even sets the house on fire," Judith said. I recalled Xan once more. Judith recalled an incident fourteen years earlier when she helped counsel a teenage boy who had been arrested for arson though he was never found with matches or any other means of starting a fire in his possession. He denied setting fires and was exonerated one evening when, in the presence of witnesses, his mattress suddenly burst into flame.

A shiver ran down my back.

Contrary to the glut of popular horror movies that seem to be based on such incidents, Judith said such children are seldom aware of their power. The phenomenon, which Judith believes occurs no more frequently than perhaps once in every 100,000 teenagers, divided equally between boys and girls, is not evidence of any special psychic ability. From her experience, there is no way the aberrant energy can be controlled or its possessor trained to use it.

It is repressed energy, she explained. The child is attempting to deal with problems maturely, unemotionally. But that repressed energy must be released somehow. Some children get rid of it on the football field, others get ulcers. In a few rare cases, the victim busts up the house without even knowing it.

Judith suggested that her caller have a heart-to-heart talk with her son. "Don't try to get him to admit having anything to do with the strange disturbances," she urged, "since he probably won't have any idea what you're talking about. Just let him know that it's all right to discuss problems and questions openly, that suppressing his anxiety is neither adult nor safe."

Judith found that once a child is able to identify and then explore emotions without fear of ridicule or retribution, the phenomena usually disappear.

"But if that doesn't do the trick," she tells clients faced with similar problems, "don't worry as long as the manifestations don't harm anyone or anything priceless. The teen will eventually grow out of it, often in as little as a couple of weeks, as his chemical balance is restored."

"All a parent really has to worry about is whether his or her pocketbook and sanity will weather the storm," Judith said.

Judith was less successful in helping me unravel a different kind of mystery, one that in its own way was as unnerving to me as Xan's prepubescent bout with unconscious pyromania.

It began with an incident the day Marty Stevens and I visited our new friend Phyllis.

"Nursing is loving and caring," Phyllis had been saying in her clipped Canadian accent. "It is so much more than machines and technology. A nurse must touch her patient, really touch him. They've gotten away from that, you know."

Phyllis was describing an article she'd authored that had set the medical community on its ear. The article, "Nursing, Love or Lore," was published in a medical journal.

"I made a lot of people angry," she said with a small smile as she recalled. "They didn't want to hear it in my article. But they listened. In the end they had me address a big conference of doctors and nurses. When I finished, you could hear a pin drop."

We were startled into the present by the appearance of Phyllis's companions, Dorothy and Elinor. Lunch was ready, she said, and led the way to an elegant spread of chicken salad in lettuce cups, plates of fresh fruit, homemade biscuits with honey and real English tea in antique china cups.

As I watched the sun streaming through the window,

turning Phyllis's white curls into a silver halo, it dawned on me that I had left my notebook in the car. I excused myself and ran out to get it since I hate to be without something to jot down thoughts when I'm talking with someone about the paranormal. I just knew where I'd find my pad. Marty and I had been flipping through some notes earlier in a nearby restaurant, then I had tossed the notebook onto the dashboard.

At that stage, there had been nothing in the pad except notes. Marty and I both agreed on that point later. Yet when I laid the pad on the table after I fetched it from the car, a sepia-colored photograph fluttered from it to the floor. I picked up the picture, puzzling over how it found its way into my note pad. Brittle with age, it revealed three men in what appeared to be U.S. Army uniforms of World War I vintage, arms around each other, smiling into the camera.

"Where'd this come from?" I wondered aloud, turning the picture for Marty's inspection.

That's when Phyllis, who was sitting across from Marty, gasped, "Why, that man on the end is Richard Paylin Thompson. I was once engaged to be married to him and have so wished to have a picture of him. He's been dead for many years. I heard that his brother died in Texas several weeks ago and have been thinking of Richard a lot lately. I loved him very much."

She didn't say why they never married.

And at that moment, I couldn't bring myself to ask.

None of us could explain the source of the picture Phyllis now clutched, as if afraid someone might try to take it away, gazing at the images printed on it and exclaiming over them. None of us could remember having seen it before.

On impulse, I grabbed a pen and began scratching on my notepad. Though I usually avoid automatic writing because I find it impossible to totally accept the concept, I found that without the words having formed in my conscious mind, I had written "PERSHING," then "BLACKJACK" and finally "BACKWARD SADDLE."

I had no idea what any of it meant.

"PERSHING and BLACKJACK are easy," said Elinor. "Obviously, they're references to Black Jack Pershing, the general. He was commander of the American forces during World War I."

And Marty was sure there was a horse named Black Jack in the funeral for President John F. Kennedy. "That was the name of the riderless horse with the boots backward in the stirrups to indicate its rider had died," she explained.

"But what does it all mean?" I wondered.

We talked about it a long time. But none of us ever came up with a reasonable theory.

Knowing these three ladies on occasion went to the race track, I jokingly suggested that if a horse named Black Jack is running, I'd bet on it.

Not even friends like Judith, who have been researching the paranormal nearly all their lives, can explain to me exactly what happened that day. There seems to be no rational explanation for the seeming coincidences that afternoon—the sudden discovery of the photograph followed by the cryptic notes scrawled in my notepad.

Perhaps the words "BACKWARD SADDLE" were intended to indicate that the message came from the dead. I like to think so, anyway. I like to believe that love still binds Phyllis with her Richard Paylin Thompson.

I talked to Phyllis several days after the incident. She too remained puzzled. But she had taken my advice, she said.

"My advice?"

"About the race track," Phyllis said. Phyllis and Dorothy had bundled up and headed for Longacres where, lo and behold, there was a horse in the running by the name of Black Jack. He turned out to be an 8-1 long shot who streaked to the finish line ahead of the pack and with a sizeable bet by Phyllis and Dorothy riding on him.

I guess some things have no logical explanation!

CHAPTER 12

There you have it. My evolution, my instant in time. I want to prolong it. I want to learn to communicate with dolphins. I want to experience the multitude of psychic phenomena I have heard described, but have never seen first hand.

Again and again, I want to feel the exhilaration—the "Oh, Wow!" if you will—of discovery, the fascination of musing over where it all begins. And where it ends.

Once, while reading in a Seattle nightclub, I told a woman she was pregnant. Her husband scoffed until his wife said, "It's true. I was going to break the news tonight. That's why I asked you to take me out to dinner."

Suddenly, I knew the month the baby was due, the fact that it would be a girl and even the name she would be given. The woman verified that the name she had in mind was Heather.

I called across the room to Barb. "Give me a name."

"Heather," she called back without hesitation. She couldn't possibly have overheard—she was 30 yards away, on the other side of a crowded, noisy restaurant.

Dr. Shafica Karagulla wrote a book called, *Breakthrough to Creativity*, in which she refers to abilities she calls "higher sense perception." Dr. Karagulla, a neuro-psychiatrist, believes there are those among us, a group she calls super-sane, who are able to adjust to a world which science now knows is not solid, concrete and rigid, but filled with vibrant, radiant energy patterns.

She suggests that man, as the most flexible life form on the planet, is evolving with special adaptations to fit this energy field. I have evolved perhaps to the Neanderthal age. I have opened a single eye and looked at what might be. I have few answers, though I am rich in questions, many of which I have no hope of resolving in this lifetime. There seems so little left to me now.

I believe we face major earth changes in the next two decades, changes which will irrevocably alter life as we know it.

As early as 1932, Edgar Cayce warned of sweeping changes in the late 1980s. Devastating volcanoes were but one type of catastrophe he foresaw transforming the faces of the entire continents.

Archeologist-anthropologist-geologist Jeffrey Goodman has pinpointed many of those changes in his book, *We Are the Earthquake Generation*. Dr. Goodman relied on predictions by psychics working independently throughout the country to compile his book on earth changes they believe will alter civilization by the year 2000.

The scenario detailed by Dr. Goodman begins with violent earthquakes. Southwestern California becomes an island as the sea sweeps into inland valleys. Oregon, Northern California and most of Washington crumble to the ocean floor. It all culminates in a shift in the earth's polar axis, causing tidal waves that sweep across the continents.

Perhaps it sounds like bad science fiction to those who've never been haunted by such visions. Those of us who have seen the world collapsing around us find them all too real, however. We compare notes on the safe spots and pray our nightmares will not come true.

Recently, I have been watching the floor beneath the Pacific Ocean, between California and Hawaii, shifting ominously. The images flood my conscious during daily meditation. And they scare the hell out of me.

Yet, I believe man will survive the catastrophes that await us. I believe there is hope, that there are spirit guides destined to lead us through the malaise and that there are now among us mortal guides who will help save, then reshape humanity.

Whether I will see it remains a mystery.

I have been with Xan a lot lately.

In a particular memorable dream, he revealed to me a headstone.

I felt like Ebeneezer Scrooge as I examined the legend carved into the stone and discovered the grave beneath belonged to me. My termination date is only three years away.

Mind of mind, I asked if this then was to be my end. At first he did not answer. Then he revealed to me a gigantic golden head in a cave I believe exists in the Andes. The head looked like a busy ant hill as human shapes glided in and out through hidden passageways. I sensed it was some sort of highly technological command center. Its purpose I cannot guess.

"You are destined to make acceptable that which will come," Xan said, "to be a bridge of knowledge, to help prepare for the devastation, to reveal that help is at hand from within and without."

I just hate it when he talks in circles like that.

I guess only the calendar will tell whether what was written on the grave is what will be. Like Old Scrooge, I'll have to do the best I can with whatever I have left.

And if death cuts short, I'll just have to learn to live with it.

Few serious psychics deny that the gift they possess comes from God. At least I have never met one.

It's true there have been those who babble and dabble in the so-called black arts, who believe evil was more powerful than good; just as there have been popes who willed holy wars. There also is an army of hucksters charading as mystics whose real values center on common stock and carpeting.

For most of us, however, the gift is sacred. We survive

as much for it as by it. We charge fees for our services, just as an artist charges for the product of his talent. When a client can't pay, we do it free.

Our role models are men like Edgar Cayce, the seer of Virginia Beach. There is little doubt, even among skeptics, that Cayce had the gift of prophecy as well as the gift of healing. And though he has been dead since 1945, his spirit survives in all of us.

Yet it survives in none more vividly than in a woman who introduced herself to me by letter during the summer of 1979. Her name is Phyllis—she asked that her last name not be published—and she lives near Seattle.

She had invited me and my colleague, Marty Stephens, to lunch and waited at the door as we walked along a front fence draped with roses, then up the path through immaculately groomed lawns to a cottage Phyllis shares with two companions.

Eyes the color of a mountain lake smiled warmly as she held the door for us.

Phyllis is 81, but hardly a doddering old woman.

The centerpiece on the large desk in her study is an electric typewriter. The walls are lined with books ranging from medical texts to Eastern philosophy to poetry. Her files are filled with manuscripts of articles, short stories, even a novel.

Though trained in science and medicine, she is a proponent of holistic medicine and has a guru from the Far East whom she believes in implicitly. A registered nurse and hospital administrator for many years, she is given to strong opinions and doesn't hesitate to share them.

Edgar Cayce is the object of many of those opinions. For two years, Phyllis assisted Cayce. She adored him, she says, but snorts derisively at his worship by many of his followers.

"He was not the elevated saint they would have the world believe," she said emphatically, hinting that he would have been ill at east with beatification. "He was a very gifted man, but he had all the foibles any man has. He had a particularly violent temper. Why, I've seen him throw books across the room in a rage. He struggled for many years with personal problems and, at times, his gift filled him with total despair. People demanded so much of him with their illnesses and their cries for help."

She paused to reflect, her voice softening.

"Perhaps there was something saintly about Edgar for he never let anyone down, never turned anyone away who could not pay," she said. "He really used his gift to heal. But he was no saint."

Then again, who among us is?

Even the saints were human. But like Cayce, they were a little closer to spiritual perfection than most. And now their spirits drift through the planes of reality, returning to us from time to time to guide and direct those who shape the course of modern history.

My friend Judith Ballard has an unusual talent. Judith, who is an artist, can sketch spirit guides. She requires no description, just the presence of the individual whose guide is to be drawn. I believe we all possess a spirit guide, though some are not as forward as Xan—or perhaps others don't need their guides as badly as I seem to need mine. Those of us who have seen our guides and have seen Judith's work can attest to the fact that her drawings are unerringly accurate.

What fascinates me about the sketches is the rich variety in the features represented. They run the gamut from haloed figures resembling paintings of saints to Oriental-looking monks to Islamic holy men to American Indians to faces that are not of this world. No single culture seems to have all the theological answers.

Judith's psychic talents were discovered when she was still a teenager. At 15, she was assisting her scientist brother in ESP research. He recognized her potential and for two years directed every step of her psychic development. At 17, she had demonstrated 19 psychic abilities, including precognition (seeing the future), clairvoyance (seeing objects in another location), clair-audience (psychic hearing) and astral travel or out-of-body experience.

Judith became disenchanted with psychic phenomena when her talents attracted the attention of a widely respected psychic who invited her to join him in his work. He exploited his talents, reducing it to little more than a magic show, she complained.

For a long time, she avoided the paranormal and anyone involved in it. But she couldn't contain her curiosity. She began meditating and reading everything she could find on the subject, developing an immense personal library.

But handwriting analysis became the love of her life. She privately published her theories on graphology and began teaching the nation's only academically accredited course on the subject. She also developed a technique she believes could enable the blind to learn to see through their fingers.

I watched in amazement as Judith gave a spontaneous demonstration over lunch in a Seattle restaurant one day. She laid a magazine on the table before a guest I had brought along, a complete stranger to Judith.

"Is there a picture on the page?" she asked the blindfolded subject as he ran his fingers over it.

"I think so."

"Yes or no?" Judith demanded—she insists on exact answers when teaching eyeless sight or finger reading.

Other diners left their food untouched as she proceeded. They seemed fascinated as I, when our guest correctly located colors, defined shapes and described people in the picture. He was not 100% accurate in his reading, but he was consistent enough that Judith pronounced him "definitely teachable."

Sightless reading is a technique Judith developed independently shortly before the Soviets announced astonishing success in research into the phenomena in 1962.

A Russian woman had developed skin reading and

was using it to teach the blind to "see." She became an overnight sensation as scientists from all over the U.S.S.R. rushed to test her. At first they hypothesized that the skin has delicate sensors that measure the temperature of colors. (Sensitive instruments have determined that there are slight temperature variations in all the colors of the spectrum, with red the warmest and blue the coolest). That theory was soon invalidated when other subjects were also trained to read print and "see" the smallest detail in pictures. They were able to pick out such things as earrings on a woman in a complex photo and buttons on a man's shirt. Soon, half the world was getting into the act. Everyone wanted to do it.

Judith believes in plunging her sightless reading students directly into complex materials.

"Magazines are perfect," she says. "The bold colors and shapes in advertising layouts provide the material I give beginners."

The object in learning this technique is to discipline the mind to screen out everything but specifics, she says. The fingers will pick up only fragments. The mind must sort them out, add them up and come up with a total.

Sometimes, though, people receive mistaken impressions. One of her students "saw" a man carrying a yellow surfboard, Judith recalls with a laugh, when in reality, the picture he was "seeing" was a banana—his fingers saw the shape and color but he didn't add up the details correctly.

Judith had been teaching skin reading since the early 1960's when physicist Helmut Schmidt discovered her. Schmidt, who was in charge of a government-sponsored ESP project at Boeing in Seattle, hired Judith and four of her students as assistants in parapsychological research. The project was to test precognition, or seeing into the future.

Judith's skin reading ability came as a surprise to Schmidt, who checked with other researchers around the country and found that no one else knew anything about it. Before he could institute a research project, the Soviets published their findings.

From 1966 to 1968, Judith and her students worked with Schmidt on the Boeing ESP project. Many were tested, but for nearly a decade Judith held the world record in ESP tests conducted under clinical conditions.

"Dr. Schmidt sat each of us in front of a machine he had developed, the Random Selector Generator," she says. "We were to guess at which of the series of lights would light up first." The responses were fed into a computer. All subjects were tested from 500 to 5,000 times for precognitive ability. The results were later published in several scientific journals.

It is fitting that scientific research should bring Judith a modicum of fame since it was scientific research which unlocked her rare gifts. She hopes one day it will also enable her to determine if her techniques can, in fact, give tactile sight to the sightless.

She and Schmidt had hoped to explore the questions, but he moved on to become Director of Research at the J.B. Rhine Foundation at Durham, N.C., then to an ESP research position in Texas.

"It takes a lot of money to conduct the kind of research that would be necessary," says Judith. "But who's going to give it to some crackpot who believes you can see with your hands?"

I am baffled by the persistent conflict between science and psychic phenomena and the battle between religion and the paranormal. Why is it so hard to believe that things we do not understand exist?

We see a rainbow and though most of us don't understand the principles of light refraction, we willingly accept that it is there. We are urged by religion to strive to be like God—not necessarily God-like, but like him in qualities we can attain. I believe this is the purpose of living again and again, to learn from our mistakes in past lives and to improve with each regeneration.

Why then, the skeptics might ask, does there con-

tinue to be so much violence and ignorance in the
world? The answer seems obvious—some of us are just
slow learners. But there is a less obvious possibility—
there are new souls being generated all the time.

At the same time, there is a small number of souls
graduating from the life cycle, souls which have won
their freedom from the hell of mortality. These have
earned a level of purity which binds them with that
omnipotent force we call God—they become God-like in
the most literal sense.

I am aware that what I believe is not a revolutionary
concept. But it is one which has taken me a long time to
understand and accept. And it definitely makes a lot
more sense to me than genocide in the name of salvation, witch hunts, weekend Christianity, intolerance
and refusal to develop our talents or to allow others to
do so.

TESTING YOUR PSYCHIC ABILITIES

Our society is perpetually bombarded by visual stimuli—movies, magazines and television—which may have been allowed to rob our ability to visualize. We have become mentally lazy, and in the process some among us have lost the capacity to see through our mind's eye.

The ability to visualize is not a prerequisite to psychic skill, but it makes it easier. Research has demonstrated that those who can visualize generally score higher on ESP tests.

This visualization exercise will help you relax and warm up your mind, while at the same time develop that part of your brain that enables visualization.

Sit comfortably in a quiet, dimly-lit room. Close your eyes and breathe deeply. Relax.

Envision before you an apple, the largest, reddest apple you have ever seen. Notice how the luster stands out against the black background. Turn the apple slowly around so you may examine the skin, its texture and coloration, from all sides. See how the stem disappears into the top, how the flesh of the fruit tapers as it descends to its puckered base. Reach out an imaginary hand and study the firmness of the fruit; bring it close to your nose so you can inhale the intoxicating scent. Now, without breaking the skin, taste the juicy fruit, feel its sweetness splash against your tongue as the sounds of a childhood summer, leaves stirred by restless breezes and bees buzzing somewhere far away, flow gently through your brain.

When you are calm and completely relaxed, proceed with the test.

The source of psychic power remains a mystery. No one has yet determined where the clairvoyant message comes from, how thoughts can be transmitted from one person to another telepathically, or what enables some among us to literally control a toss of the dice.

It is a question as old as man's fascination with the occult, yet as new as the ongoing debate over whether parapsychology is in fact a legitimate science.

It is my belief that you can train your brain to be more psychic. It does involve mental exercises, and like all exercises you should pace yourself. Do a little each day and soon you will find a heightened state of awareness.

Please remember that exertion is physically demanding. Done properly, these tests require extreme concentration which could leave you feeling as if you had spent a day in the office or eight hours in a coal mine. Attempting more than one type of test at a single sitting is not only tiring, but can have a negative effect on your test results.

Precognition is the ability to forecast the future. The objective of this test is to determine whether you can foresee the order in which cards will come out of a shuffled deck.

Materials include a Rhine deck, a notebook for keeping scores over an extended period and a tablet for recording answers during the test.

On your note pad write down the symbols of the 25 cards in the Rhine deck in the order you believe they will be dealt. Next shuffle the cards and one at a time turn them over, recording on the note pad the actual order in which they are dealt. Compare the two lists for correct guesses. Repeat the test five more times.

Scores are based on the 150 guesses with a chance factor of 30. Consistent scores of 40 or more correct guesses per 150, or 20 or less correct guesses per 150, are noteworthy.

Psychokinesis is the ability to move, control or otherwise affect physical objects using nothing more tangible than mental energy. The objective of this test is to control the toss of dice.

Materials include a single die, a notebook for keeping score over an extended period, and a tablet for recording the day's results.

While shaking the die in your hand, concentrate on the number you want to come up. Though the obvious inclination is to focus on a single number time after time, researchers recommend against it, arguing that it is possible to unconsciously bias the die by learning how to throw it or what to throw it against in order to get the desired results. On your notebook, write the number you want the die to land on, then visualize that number and, finally, launch the die. Beside the number you envisioned, write the number the die landed on. Repeat the test 180 times.

Scores are based on 180 guesses, with a probability factor of 30. Consistent scores of 40 or more correct guesses per 180, or 20 or less correct per 180, are noteworthy.

If you find that you do very well in the above psychokinesis test, try it with two dice and you may be Las Vegas-bound.

I would encourage you to attempt these tests with different partners. You'll find that with some people there is a stronger psychic link. I call this an energy bridge. When you find the person who is your match on the test, be prepared for some amazing results.

When we ran an ESP test for the *Seattle Post-Intelligencer* many teachers had their students participate in the test in classrooms. The highest success rate of all the readers who participated in the test were junior high students. I am doing a research project on psychic teenagers and would like any data showing significant test results.

Telepathy is the ability to mentally send and receive messages. The objective of the test is to determine how effective you are at receiving mental images generated by another. It is recommended that you have your partner warm up just as you have done preparatory to the test.

Materials necessary are a deck of Rhine cards, which can be purchased from most book stores for less than $15 or can be made at home by using 3x5 cards with the following symbols: a circle, square, cross, star, and three wavy lines. Use a wide black felt pen for best results. You will also need a notebook in which to record the results of this and all future tests, and a tablet of clean paper for use during the test itself.

Have your partner take the Rhine deck into an adjoining room, completely out of your sight, but within hearing. Have him shuffle the deck thoroughly, then, one at a time, lift the top card and concentrate all of his energy on the card. Write it in your tablet, then orally signal your partner to proceed to the next card. It is important to write down the first image that comes to mind. Do not attempt to bring it into clear focus and do not allow your mind to wander to such topics as the odds of whether your "guess" is going to be right. One of the best ways to ruin your score is to keep track of the cards. Forget your previous guesses and make each new one as if it is your first. If you feel in your bones that every card has a circle on it, guess circle every time. Just don't base any guess on how you guessed last time. Once you have completed the deck, check your guesses against the cards, which should have been stacked in order as they were handled by your partner. Repeat the test five more times. Scores are based on laws of probability and require that you go through several runs—a minimum of six per sitting—in order to gather substantive data. Six times through the deck will give you 150 guesses upon which to base your evaluation. Probability dictates that out of the 150 guesses you will have 30 correct answers. Variations grow in significance as they progress above or below 30—even a score significantly below chance can be an indication of strong psychic power, according to researchers. Consistent scores of 40 or more correct guesses per 150 or 20 or less correct guesses per 150 are noteworthy.

Psychometry is the ability to derive information from objects merely by touching them. The objective of the test is to measure your psychometric talent.

Materials include a Rhine deck, a notebook for keeping scores over an extended period and a tablet for recording answers during the test.

In a horizontal line before you, lay out one of each of the five different Rhine cards—waves, square, cross, star and a circle—face up. Shuffle the remaining cards, then take the top card from the deck and holding it face down, place it on the upturned card you think it matches. It is important to respond instinctively. Do not rationalize or contemplate the odds. Put the card on a stack as soon as you sense it belongs there. Proceed through the deck in this manner, then turn the cards over to see how accurate you were in placing them and write the results on your tablet. Repeat the test nine more times.

Scores are based on 200 guesses with a probability factor of 40. Consistent scores of 50 or more correct guesses per 200 or 30 or less correct guesses per 200 are noteworthy.

Visualizing Colors: This test gauges the skill of the "sender" as well as the "receiver" and requires great concentration on the part of each.

Begin by making a deck of six cards by cutting white cardboard into two-by-four-inch rectangles. Now attach a colored circle—red, orange, yellow, green, blue or purple—to the middle of each card. The "sender" shuffles the cards with his back to the "receiver," then turns one up and studies it. He shuts his eyes and visualizes it while the "receiver" concentrates on a circle and imagines it being colored in. He then names the color.

This test should be done at least twenty-four times if it is to yield pertinent data. Any score of four out of twenty-four is significant. This is an easy test for parents to give young children—reward their efforts with raisins.

Willpower: This is a great party game, since many of us find it easier to open up in social situations.

One person leaves the room while the others select an object in the room to concentrate on. When the test subject returns he is willed in the direction of the object, which he must identify. He should pay no attention to anything except his own hunches.

Telepathic Elimination: After laying six playing cards face down in a row, he then tells the receiver the card but not its position in the row. The receiver turns up the cards, one by one, trying not to turn up the chosen card. If the chosen card is not among the first three the subject is credited with a successful score. This test should be done forty-eight times if it is to yield pertinent data. Any score over twenty for forty-eight is signifcant. This test should be done daily. Compare your beginning score with one two weeks later to see how well you have learned to hone up your telepathic power.

Group Reception: The sender writes a two-digit number in clear, large numerals. He sits under a bright light and studies the written number by half closing his eyes, then slowly opens them at intervals. Other members of the group sit with pads and pencils. Each tries to gain an impression of the number and writes it on his paper. The odds are 90-1 against success. If two receivers have identical numbers not sent by the sender, they should take additional tests without the rest of the group.

Time Test: This can be done by two persons or a group. Use a watch that is not running. Set the watch at five to or five after the hour—any hour—but don't tell anyone what the watch is set on. Then place the watch under an inverted cup with the cup handle on a direct line with the watch stem so the receiver or receivers can visualize the exact position of the hidden watch. Receivers then try to tell the time on the watch. The odds against picking the correct time is 144 to 1. One hundred tries are necessary to yield pertinent data—two correct answers out of 100 is significant.

Pick the Card: This test is excellent for use with young children. Lay a deck of cards face down on the floor and ask the child to find a red lady and black man. Reward correct answers with praise and/or a small treat. Done ten minutes a day, this helps youngsters develop psychic abilities.

VISUALIZING COLORS

Everyone has felt the effects of color—the foreboding of black, the excitement of red, the buoyancy of yellow. Few would argue its ability to influence both mental and physical health.

Despite the volumes that have been written on color therapy, however, little attention has been given to a favorite of mine, color breathing. The name itself is certain to conjure up all sorts of distasteful images for those of you who have been stuck on a crowded elevator with a fat man with halitosis. Erase that image from your mind and instead visualize yourself inhaling the redness of a rose or the blueness of a summer sky.

Visualization is important in enabling you to use color to awaken your psychic awareness. If you have trouble visualizing in color, exercise your mind a few minutes each day. Take a towel, a blanket, a sheet of paper, any object of the desired hue, just be sure the object is a solid color—no checks or plaids or polka dots. Concentrate on the color with your eyes open, then with your eyes closed. Soon you will find that you no longer need the prop to create the color in your mind's eye.

You will have to decide for yourself which color is best for you. Remember that there are many shades to each so you may have to shop around awhile before you find the one that's just right. Pretend you have captured a rainbow and now must sort through those strands of brilliance for the one that touches your soul.

I breath pink every morning. Pink is the color of universal love. It gives joy and comfort and has a calming effect that aids in meditation. It is a color that appeals to me, both physically and emotionally.

To help you better understand the implications of the color you select, Linda Clark offers some marvelous insights in her book, *The Ancient Art of Color Therapy.* Below are a few common colors and their meanings—perhaps yours will be among them:

Red is the color of vibrant energy. Breathe red when you're feeling low or anemic. Concentrate on the area around your heart as you inhale its warmth. But avoid breathing red just before you go to bed or you'll never get to sleep.

Yellow is the color of healing. Its sunshine takes away aches and pains and leaves in their place a feeling of contentment.

Blue is the color of rest and relaxation. It could be considered an opposite of red. It soothes away pains like those of migraines. But avoid blue in the morning or you're liable to wind up falling back to sleep.

Orange combines the qualities of the colors that go to produce it, red and yellow. It brings both healing and energy, relieving respiratory disorders and muscle cramps. But like red, it can be too exciting for bedtime breathing, especially if it is a hot, red-orange. If you must use orange at bedtime, make it the color of the sunset.

Green combines the qualities of yellow and blue, making it both relaxing and therapeutic. It is the color of rejuvenation. It is naturally a quiet loving color favored by many hospitals.

Violet combines the qualities of red and blue to create a sense of soothing energy. It you're in a good mood, this is a fantastic color for breathing, but stay away if you are even mildly depressed or you could find yourself on a real downer.

Black is the absence of all color. It is an ominous shadow. Avoid breathing it unless the only fictional character with whom you have ever felt real empathy is the Phantom of the Opera.

White combines the qualities of all colors to create purity, the psychic umbrella which wards off negativity. When you are angry with someone or something or feel others are angry with you, breathe white. It will make you feel much better and it won't hurt anyone else either.

Once you have chosen your color, the act of breathing it is easy. Imagine before you a translucent ball of color, a round cloud, so to speak. As you slowly inhale, it comes toward you until it is sucked in through your nostrils. Your mind's eye watches as it swirls along the windpipe, then fills the lungs with its richness. Now exhale slowly, noticing that the cloud is darker as it escapes your lungs, carrying with it the impurities of your flesh and your soul. Once in the air, however, the impurities evaporate away and leave behind the pure sphere of color, ready once more to be inhaled into your lungs.

Breathe away your troubles for five minutes each day and see if the color doesn't come back to your cheeks, not to mention your disposition.

POSTSCRIPT

There are no accidents. Everything happens for a reason. You may not know why you must endure pain, but once you have endured it and look back, if you are able to look back with some measure of objectivity, you generally realize that the trauma brought with it reward.

In the paranormal, there is a favorite adage: When the student is *ready*, the teacher appears.

But the adage doesn't always come in the form of a single person. It may be several people, each contributing to the answer. Or even a book or a series of books or some seemingly innocuous message over the television or radio. It can even come in the form of a scrap of overheard conversation.

Usually, it comes when it is most needed. By 1980, I had gained a local following in the Seattle area. I was hardly a household name, but I had gained recognition. I was making a comfortable living, was respected by my peers and had a growing clientele. It was in March of that year that Marty Stevens suggested in passing, that I try my hand at producing a column on the paranormal.

I didn't set out to become a psychic.

And I certainly didn't set out to be a writer.

I took a gamble and in the process met a man by the name of George Pica, an editor at the *Seattle Post-Intelligencer* who was willing to take a gamble as well.

Over the course of the next year, he invested his time and energy in helping me to say what I have to say. He gave me my first opportunity to communicate with a broad audience. In the process, he also became my severest critic and one of my dearest friends.

Friendships never happen by accident.

It was April, 1980, when my sister Jacquie undertook a bit of amateur dream analysis. I had dreamed I was standing before a blackboard on which were written the names of luminaries in psychic research; Ruth Montgomery, Brad Steiger, Gina Cenemaria, Sybil Leek. These were names that populated my library, authors whose work made up the alter at which I meditated. When I looked for answers, they often were the ones who supplied them.

And there among their names, someone had written mine on that blackboard.

When I told Jacquie about the dream, she asked, "Did you know they'll be gathering at a symposium in Oklahoma?"

She then produced a flyer that somehow had found its way into her possession.

"You've got to go," she declared, then set about figuring out how I would get there.

That symposium proved a catharsis for me. I felt an instant kinship with those I met there and that in itself became an answer. One by one, I brought most of them to Seattle to share their insights with residents of my community. And it was one of those visits that brought recognition in a bestseller by Ruth Montgomery.

Over dinner, Ruth announced that I would be among those featured in her up-coming book, *Threshold to Tomorrow.* I was flattered. Soon I would be overwhelmed. Publication of the book brought a deluge of mail from Ruth's readers.

Among those responding was a caller from Texas.

"If ever you are in my area," Jim Robinson said, " I hope to meet you."

His mother Jolene, who is affectionately called Jingles by everyone who knows her, then got on the phone.

"Would you come and be our house guest?" she asked.

And with no more than a reference in Ruth Montgomery's book and a telephone conversation to introduce us, we became instant friends. I took them up on the invitation, flew to San Antonio and discovered an entire new audience for the message I believe I was sent here to deliver.

While in Texas, I also visited Helmut Schmidt, who had worked with Judith Ballard while he was in charge of the parapsychology department of Boeing. In laboratory experiments under Dr. Schmidt's supervision, Judith had eclipsed previous world records for success in extrasensory perception.

Dr. Schmidt introduced me to a new machine, new exercises and new methods he is developing for scientific exploration of the paranormal, then asked me to participate in his research.

If it hadn't been for Judith, Jingles and Jim, it never would have happened. It was no accident.

Several major publishing houses voiced interest in this book, but all said the economy was too weak for them to take a chance on a previously unpublished author. Publish it yourself, one counseled, and demonstrate that there's a market.

I know nothing about publishing.

But Fay Marie Ainsworth does. The daughter of a lifelong friend, Fay Marie directs a specialty publishing house in the Northwest. She offered to handle the book, but like her larger counterparts, couldn't do it without some guarantee of covering the costs.

I didn't have the money.

It appeared the project would have to be scrapped.

Then Harriet Tanner heard about my dilemma. For 13 years, Harriet has been among my most loyal clients.

"I have the money," she told me.

"I can't accept it," I replied. "There's too great a risk."

"Look," she declared, "you've helped me when I needed help. And I'm darned if you will refuse me the chance to help you."

There are no accidents, only love and the rewards that come with it.

Those I have named and those I shall name here are among the multitude I love:

(X) My mother, Dorothy Teabo, who has endured an accident of birth—a daughter named Shirlee—with good humor and patience.

(X) My sister, Jacquie Witherite, who forgave me my childhood sins and has become my closest friend.

(X) Bob and Gordon—most women are fortunate if they find one good husband . . . I found two.

(X) My children, who I can say in all honesty and affection never gave me a moment's peace, but more times than they will ever know, gave me three good reasons for living.

(X) Alice Fisher, who gave me Alaska, and Lucille and Gill Gillham and Beryl Motzkus, who came with it.

(X) Lenore Small, Jack and Barbara Atkinson, who worked like slaves and were paid in the same way.

(X) Barb Easton, who is a constant source of tranquility, and in my opinion, one of the nation's best psychics.

(X) Larry Dieffenbach, who is a source of salvation.

(X) Pinckney Ferguson and Jackie Cramer, who contributed to the fact that this book actually made it to the press.

(X) Donna Linstead for bailing me out of down moods with her crazy humor.

(X) Ruth Montgomery, just for being Ruth Montgomery. (A guiding light to us all.)

(X) Brad Steiger, for being an inspiration and a friend.

I can never repay the gifts these and others, whose names would fill yet another volume, have given. But there is an adage which holds that the best way to repay a kindness from one person is to do a kindness for another. For that reason, I offer you this single fact of life.

We are all psychics under the skin.

I realize that if I convince enough of you that this fact is true, I may be well on my way to putting myself out of business.

But it's true.

And to prove it, I would like to introduce you to six tests that will help you exercise your psychic muscle. These and other fascinating tests were collected in 1944 by Joseph Dunninger and published in *What's On Your Mind?*, copies of which are available at many public libraries if you'd like to explore your telepathic powers more thoroughly.

The only rules are:

A. Don't clutch. Nobody's taking grades, though you may want to compare your scores with those of your friends.

B. And give the first answer that comes to mind— follow your instinct. Don't try to focus images in your mind; you'll just confuse yourself and your score.

And there you have it. At most, a glimpse at the evolution of a psychic, a moment in time.

Thank you for spending that moment with me.